From the
Ground Up

From the
Ground Up

JOHN P. COUTIS

MACMILLAN
Pan Macmillan Australia

John P. Coutis's website can be visited at:
www.becauzewecan.com

First published 2001 in Macmillan by Pan Macmillan Australia Pty Limited
St Martins Tower, 31 Market Street, Sydney

National Library of Australia
Cataloguing-in-Publication data:

Coutis, John P.
From the ground up.

ISBN 0 7329 1068 4.

1. Coutis, John. 2. Handicapped – Australia – Biography.
3. Lecturers – Australia – Biography. I. Armstrong, Geoff.
II. Title.

305.908166

Typeset in Life Roman by Post Pre-press Group
Printed in Australia by McPherson's Printing Group

Cover and text design by Liz Seymour, Seymour Designs
Front cover photograph courtesy of Premier Studio, Western Australia.
Back cover photograph: John Coutis at the National Young Leaders' Day.
Courtesy of Highlife Education Ltd.

To my parents Gary and Evelyn Coutis
I am who I am because of you. Without you I would not
be living the life I am today. Your courage to 'break the
rules' and take me home saved my life. You are my rock,
there for me with wisdom, encouragement, love and a big
shove or hug when I need it most. I owe you everything.

To my best friend Matthew Anderson (1972–1996)
For being the first to tell me to write a book and giving
me the title *From the Ground Up* to get me started –
I finally did it, mate.

To my wife Trish van Leeuwen
Without you this book may never have happened. Thank
you for all your understanding, encouragement and love.
You are my soul mate and best friend. I love you with all
my heart. Together and doing it our way.

Motivation lasts for 10 minutes . . .
inspiration lasts a lifetime.

Foreword

Whenever I think of John Coutis, two words immediately spring to mind – 'boofhead' and 'legend'. Many others follow soon after, including 'inspirational', 'energetic', 'uplifting', 'motivational', 'humorous', 'adventurous' and 'generous'.

One word that certainly doesn't belong in any sentence about Johnno is 'disabled'. In fact, it's the last five letters of that adjective that are spot on.

The only time I ever saw John as being different was the first time I laid eyes on him, at a hotel in the outer Sydney suburb of Windsor in the early 1990s. I had to blink twice when I saw what looked to be a human crab scurry across the pub floor, launch itself onto a bench and from there, in a split second, up onto the bar to order two Southern

Comfort and Cokes. He then shoved one of the drinks down his shirt while carrying the other in his hand, hopped back down onto the floor and sped over to his mates. I just had to meet this guy.

From the very first moment I met John, I knew he was no ordinary person. Rather, he was a special bloke destined to enlighten many people. He has the gift of the gab, that precious ability to communicate with anyone and everyone, and bring out their best. Children gravitate to him as if he were the Pied Piper, while adults are always left feeling much more positive for having crossed his dynamic path.

Johnno's destiny is to make people realise that life isn't so bad and that if you really set your mind to it, you can achieve just about anything. Johnno himself has overcome not only the physical limitations he has faced since birth (though he still can't play golf), he has also fought a number of personal battles – especially with his health – and won every time because of his fierce determination and an iron will to succeed. This was especially true through late 1999 and 2000, when he had to endure a frightening battle with cancer, and then straight after his wedding in July 2000, when his physical condition again took a turn for the worse.

I could go on endlessly with my favourite Johnno tales, but I think I should leave the storytelling to him in the pages that follow. And anyway, I don't want to give him a bigger head than he already has by giving him too many wraps! However, there is one story I can't let slip by.

Johnno tells it himself in the chapter 'Part of a Team', but I'd like to add my two bob's worth here . . .

It happened during John's first overseas trip with the Australian cricket team, to South Africa back in early 1994. Being a bit wet behind those not insignificant ears and unaccustomed to the luxuries of five-star accommodation, the boy from North Richmond couldn't believe his luck as we settled into our luxurious lodgings in Johannesburg. Not only were there numerous TV stations and movies, as well as room service, laundry pick-up and wake-up calls, there was also a wide range of opulent facilities in the bathroom. In one corner was the shower, adjacent was the bath, across from it was the toilet and a vanity basin, and next to the toilet, unbelievably Johnno must have thought, was another basin, seemingly specifically designed for the disabled. Now, as I've explained, Johnno isn't disabled in my eyes, or his, but when he looked at that basin he must have reckoned, well, bewdy, this'll make life a bit easier.

Soon after checking out his room, Johnno got the call to tidy up and refresh himself before dinner. Moments later the hotel porter came to his room to drop off John's bags and moments after that there was a commotion, and more than a little yelling and cursing, coming from Johnno's bathroom.

What caused the commotion? I'll leave that for Johnno to describe. But one thing that confuses me is that, as he tells it, he was quick to 'fess up to his mistake. As I remember it, despite the rumours that swept the team, it took the boofhead the best part of a week before he came clean. 'I thought it tasted a bit like detergent,' he quietly admitted.

I know there will be plenty more Johnno stories in the years to come, just as I know he will positively affect the lives of thousands more with his optimism and his strength of character. These positive traits, perhaps above all the others, are always an inspiration to me.

Steve Waugh
April 2001

Contents

Acknowledgments

THIS BOOK HAS EVENTUATED because of the demand from all the fabulous people I meet speaking and who cross my path every day. So many of you have at one time or another told me to write my story because you want to take a little piece of me home to share with your family. Thank you for encouraging me to share my story in a book.

Anyone who knows anything about success, knows it is the unconditional support and love from many people who help you get there. This book would not have made it off the press without a huge thanks to the following people.

Geoff Armstrong, writer, researcher, editor and the one who has helped me the most to get my story on paper.

Thanks, Geoff, for your patience, perseverance and passion for this book and your belief in my story.

Tom Gilliatt, Bernadette Foley, Briony Cameron and all the crew at Pan Macmillan, who were convinced I had a story after I spent a meeting walking around on their boardroom table. (I am not sure they knew what they were letting themselves in for.) You are a great team of professionals who have given the book its polish and finish.

To friends who endured telephone calls, interviews and visits to collect background information for the book. Thank you Alan Jones, Lisa Curry-Kenny, Tom O'Toole, Gavin and Kath Robertson, Joe Hutton and Dr Warrick MacKay. Each of you has made a huge contribution to my life and are a special part of it.

Special thanks to Stephen Waugh, one of Australia's finest sportsmen, who I am honoured to call one of my best friends. Thanks, champ, for your contribution to this book, my career and for your unconditional friendship and support on and off the field.

An extra big thank you to professional photographers Janet Craig from Premier Studio (WA) and Max Ucherek from Fern Fine Photography (NSW) for allowing me to use photos they have taken.

I am lucky in my professional life to have terrific corporate backing from ASICS, BOLLE, Mensland, the DVG Group (Perth, WA), WIN TV, Knightwriter Productions and the Parramatta Leagues Club. Each company provides me with the tools to present me at my best in public, thank you for your unquestioning support.

To Adam, Leonie, Kimberley, Amanda, Harrison, Luke, Kristy and Liberty Coutis, you make up the core of my very precious family. To my extended family Hans, Anna, Debbie, Brett, Mitchell, Ryleigh, Gerald and Kimberley, thank you for allowing me to be part of your lives and for your support. To all my family and friends, you are very important to me and I love each of you very much.

My aim every day is to be the best person I can be. If I can inspire just one person every day to also be the best they can be, to love their life and who they are, to accept and meet life's challenges head on, and to believe in themselves and stand tall, then it has been a great day.

Look beyond what you see in front of you. Believe in others, yourself and life.

John P. Coutis

Prologue

THESE DAYS I MAKE my living as a public speaker. And what's the first thing you notice when I walk out on-stage? I have no legs. I usually emerge from behind a curtain, rolling in on my skateboard, my gloved hands propelling me towards a chair perched on the front of the stage. From there, often leaving that chair to roam around the stage and sometimes stopping to crack a joke with someone in the audience, I offer my message, which – in very basic terms – is that if I can, you can. As I often say, 'Everyone is born with a disability. The difference with my disability is that you can see it.'

You must be positive about life, I tell the assembly. Change what you don't want in your life. Take advantage of what's right. Enjoy the struggle. Love the people around you and enjoy their love for you. Love life.

If I can, you can.

For many years I didn't think I could make a difference to how others approached their lives, handled their pressures, coped with their insecurities. To be frank, when I started my public speaking I was very sceptical. I was worried about how people would see me – as someone worth listening to or just a freak of nature, a sideshow to the main event. About whether they'd listen, about whether my words would have an impact.

In one of my first gigs, I was on the bill at a Brad Cooper 'High Achievers' seminar. Here I was, one presenter among a collection of speakers who, all up, would be worth many millions, no, many *billions* of dollars. People such as Rodney Adler, Brad Cooper, Cathryn Duvei, Wayne Pearce, Lisa Curry-Kenny, Grant Kenny, Stefan Ackerie, Tom O'Toole and Ian Elliott.

And me, from the little provincial town of North Richmond, with my five cents' worth. I was intimidated, but what could I do but give it my very best shot? I always say you should back yourself. I stood up, tall as I could, and spoke for about 10 minutes, and managed to earn myself a standing ovation. I'll never forget how proud I felt at the end of that.

As the audience kept applauding, I didn't know what to do. 'Thanks very much, thank you, thank you . . . thank you . . . I hope I've given you something . . . thank you (c'mon, Johnno, off-stage now, mate) . . . thank you, thank you.'

A group of people came up to the stage, and I dashed down to say g'day. Some high-powered business people asked for my autograph, which I was happy to give, but it seemed so bizarre. There were a few photographs taken, a couple more autographs, and then a lady pushed herself right in front of me. The poor woman was a mess, she'd clearly been in tears and now she was crying again. It was a genuine, heartfelt plea for help.

'John,' she said, not caring about the people around us. 'Thank you for what you said today. I was going to kill myself until I saw you on stage.'

Her words didn't gel straightaway. I didn't react too seriously. 'Nuh, don't do that. Don't worry. It's lucky you're not going to do that.'

'Thank you very much,' she said, and then she went away.

I spoke to a few more people, signed some more signatures, smiled into the flashbulbs for a couple more high-flyers. And then, finally, it was time to go, but this lady was still there, waiting at the back of the auditorium.

'John,' she said quietly, 'do you mind if we go for a walk?'

'Okay,' I replied. 'No problem at all.'

We walked for ages, talking about all sorts of things but with her mainly telling me about how tough her life had become and how depressed she was, and me pushing hard my argument that her life wasn't all bad, that the answer wasn't to run away but to confront the bad parts, make changes and then have some fun. By the time we'd finished walking, I'd done more kilometres than Pat Farmer, and we ended up in her hotel room, where we sat in the comfy chairs and talked some more. And then she went over to her handbag and pulled out a gun.

There was one bullet in it.

'Thank you, John,' this woman said without a grin. 'I won't be needing this any more. I can see there are reasons to keep going.'

She handed me the gun, and I asked, 'Um, uh, what are you giving this to me for?'

And I thought, here I was, an absolute stranger to this person and yet she was trusting me and my positive philosophy with her life.

I took the bullet out and together we wrapped the gun up in one of the laundry bags you get in those flash hotel rooms. We went across the road to the beach, then along the sand to the rocks. There, out of sight, I asked this lady to throw the gun into the Pacific Ocean, which she did. And I said to her, 'Right, your life starts now. Let's start living.'

'Thank you very, very much,' she cried.

She was weeping; I was weeping. She gave me a kiss on the forehead, then a smile, a beautiful smile. I think that was the first time she'd really smiled since we met. Then she bent down and gave me another, longer kiss on the forehead, and with that she left me and walked slowly back to her room.

I stayed on those rocks and bawled my bloody eyes out.

In the Beginning

AS I SAT THERE on those Central Coast rocks, looking out over God's big, blue ocean, I was shaking and blubbering and yet, without trying to belittle that poor woman's desperate problem for even one moment, I was more than a bit proud of myself, too. For me it was like a fairytale, a dream come true. I was pinching myself and was even laughing every now and then. For the first time in my life, people were not just seeing me and staring at me, they were actually hearing me *and* listening to what I had to say. My message mattered, my opinions mattered, my humanity mattered. I had just changed the course of a life. I was such a long way from the days, many years but just a couple of decades before, when most people I encountered looked upon me as being something of a freak.

The *Macquarie Dictionary* has eight definitions for the word 'freak'. A freak, according to the *Macquarie* is:

> *2. any abnormal product or curiously unusual object; monstrosity. 3. a person or animal on exhibition as an example of some strange deviation from nature.*
> *4. a person who does not conform to orthodox, conservative forms of behaviour . . . 5. colloq. a person who is enthused about a particular thing . . .*

At different stages, in various people's eyes including my own, I have been all of these things. Today, the way I look at it, if I'm a freak it's because I've fought through a very tough battle so that I'm able to make a difference to people's lives. Not many people get to have an impact on others. Fewer still do so after encountering the stresses I've faced. But, please, don't read this and think, Gee, doesn't he think he's special.

I don't think I'm special. I reckon I'm just like everybody else. That's my point. We all have challenges in our lives, hurdles to climb, setbacks to fight back from. The difference with my disability is that you can see it. My disability hasn't stopped me from making a difference, and yours shouldn't stop you.

If I can, you can.

So who is John Coutis? I'm a little fella who was born with a severe disability, an absolute shocker. I'm a knockabout sort of bloke who was born with legs that were no good at all. They were deformed; they never worked or grew; they were screwed. I don't exactly know what happened, the doctors didn't explain it or tell me why my body turned out that way; it was just one of those things. I came into the world with my spine bent out of shape; it hadn't extended as it should have, so from the stomach down I was all out of alignment. When I sat, I did so with my little legs – which looked like they should have belonged to a frog rather than a human being – tucked underneath me. Childhood photos show me perched in a sort of swami position with my little brother towering over me.

Dr Warwick Mackay (John's family doctor since April 1987): John was born with a really gross abnormality of the very bottom of his spine. In medical terms, his disability is called congenital sacral agenesis, with spina bifida. Agenesis is where the lower part of your spine does not develop, and that's what happened with John. The sacrum [a triangular bone at the base of the spine that joins to the hipbone on either side and forms part of the pelvis] just didn't happen. He also had paraplegic symptoms in his lower limbs, and bladder and bowel abnormalities, too.

His legs had bones and all the normal tissues, but were grossly abnormal in their structure and totally useless in their function. They were very vestigial. They did grow, but not at anything like the same rate as the rest of his body. Compared to how his arms developed, they ended up about one-sixth the size of what a normal leg would have been.

I'm a bloke who wasn't expected to survive 24 hours but who has in fact lived a life full of fun, love and warmth – interrupted occasionally by some terrible mistakes and painful moments. I've been through a whole range of emotions, ups and downs; been round and round in a psychological mixer. Through it all, let me tell you, I've learnt some lessons.

I was born into a brilliantly loving family, the second son of Gary Peter Coutis and Evelyn Grace Bourke, at Blacktown Hospital on 14 August 1969. I headed straight from my mother's womb to the emergency ward; legend has it that I was no more than the size of a Coca-Cola can. It appeared that there were just too many things wrong with my body for me to survive. The doctor's advice to my father was cruel but honest – 'I'm sorry, you'll need to organise a funeral.' Fortunately Dad's pedestrian, tearful gestures to organise that service were a complete and utter waste of time. The coffin stayed in storage. I lasted the day. Then I lasted the week. Then I lasted more than 30 years. In fact, though my body looked to be a complete mess, inside I wasn't in too bad a condition, more like a near-complete jigsaw with a number of pieces in the wrong spots. The only things that were totally shot were my legs.

Gary Coutis (father): We never picked his name out. The priest at Blacktown picked his name out. He came to give John the last rites when he was born. They had to give him a name, a name to be buried with. Mum was still unconscious; I wasn't there; the baby wasn't supposed to see the day out. John and Peter were two strong names from the disciples. It was the priest that actually named him 'John Peter Coutis'. He was supposed to be 'Mark' if he was a boy.

About six weeks after I was born – after all the stress of being told that I wasn't going to last a day, two days, a week, that 'Mr Coutis, I'm sorry, you'll need to organise a funeral', that the most appropriate coffin was one the size of a shoebox – the same doctors walked up to Mum and Dad and said without warning, 'Well, good news. He's strong enough to go home.'

This was not something my parents were expecting. Until that point they had been waiting, as my Dad puts it today, for me to 'croak' it.

From what I understand, most new parents suffer from stage fright when they take their baby home from hospital. What are we going to do? How are we going to cope? What if we can't do it? Why are we doing this? I was my parents' second child, but even though they had been through the taking-new-baby-home syndrome before, can you imagine what thoughts and fears would have been buzzing through their brains on that slow drive home? My Mum and Dad had already resolved to try to raise me at home in as normal a way as possible, even though they had received and would continue to receive strong advice to the contrary. This came from friends, family and medical specialists. In some countries the advice might have been even more brutal – let's get rid of him. (There are some countries where, if you go and dig up their rubbish tips, you might find skeletons of kids who had been born with disabilities. These are kids who were like me, kids who were like you.) But back in September 1969, Mum and Dad were firm. And smart enough to recognise that just because someone has a major physical disability it doesn't mean that person is mentally disabled as well. Some people who should have been smarter didn't agree. They were wrong.

> **Evelyn Coutis (mother):** I'm one of those people who accepts things. If it happens to you, well, that's it, get on with it. They kept him in hospital for six weeks and then they wanted to put him in a home. But my husband and I just made a decision to go and get him, and we went and got him and took him home.

> **Gary Coutis:** We just took a punt, did it our way and broke the rules. We just treated John like a kid. We said, 'He's our kid. If he dies, he dies; if he doesn't, he doesn't.'

While I did survive, there were still a number of rare and ugly afflictions that I had to overcome. Apart from my useless legs and ugly melon, I didn't have an anal passage. All they could do was cut a gash to let me do painfully what most newborn babies love doing out of habit. Without that gash, my Dad reminds me from time to time, I'd have been full of shit. Sometimes he adds, with a grin, 'Maybe the operation didn't work.'

> **Liberty Coutis (grandmother):** We were really upset, but we just took it that that was the way it had to be, so we treated him like any normal child. Just because he had no legs didn't mean to say he needed to be pampered. He wasn't.
>
> At the hospital they said, 'We'll find a place to put him.' Gary and Eve said, 'No, he's coming home with us.' They had to come and inspect the house to see where Gary and Eve were going to have him, and he was brought home. Then they used to come and see he was being kept all right, because the lady told us when people get children like that, they tend to put them in a room and forget about them. So they did that a few times and saw he was being looked after well, so they didn't bother to come any more.

Why am I writing this book? I'm writing it for anyone who's struggling in some way, to give them hope and faith in themselves. I hope my story can teach such people, especially young kids who are battling away, to believe in themselves. There are so many young people, champions of the future, who see themselves with big problems. Sometimes they think that their troubles are insurmountable. But really, in most cases, their problems aren't that big. In my view, what these people need is the ability to believe in themselves, to recognise that life isn't *that* hard. Human beings are such a terrible group in the way we refuse to back ourselves. But everything *will* be okay in the long run.

I reckon the story of my experiences, my struggles, can help others recognise that anything is possible if you truly believe in yourself, your dreams and your goals. Sure, I've had a few bad times, but there has been a tremendous number of great times in my life as well. That's the story I want to share. I want people to know that no matter how different we seem, no matter what nationality we are, no matter what colour our skin is, what colour our hair is, no matter how different we look on the outside, deep down inside we are all exactly the same. Our emotions, our feelings and our hearts, they all do the same thing.

I am no different from my beautiful next-door neighbour, Grace, or my champion little mate, Mitchell, from across the road. I am no different from my father; what a great man he is! You cut me, I bleed; you tell me a sad story, I cry. We are all the same. Yes, I have a physical disability, but that's me. I've learnt to live with it, to deal with it and move on. You might need to do the same. After all, every single person has a disability in their lives – whether it be physical, mental, emotional, whatever it is – that they need to come to terms with.

Hopefully this book can change even one person's life. 'Look what he's done with his life,' I want people to say. 'If he can do what he's done after the start he had, then I can most certainly do anything I want with mine.'

No matter what you think of yourself, you *can* do it. But

you do need to believe in yourself, back your own ability. Get going before it's too late.

Today, 31 years after that gruelling day when I was born, I'm a big fella standing 78 centimetres very tall. I'm a bit of a larrikin, bit of a boofhead. But, as I said, in so many ways I'm no different from you – whether you have three kids or are never going to be a parent; whether you're out of the workforce, a train driver on your way to work, a politician in a suit, anyone.

We're all the same, every single one of us.

I don't like talking about my physical disability, so I'm certainly not going to enjoy writing about it. The way I was raised, I had no disability, or at least that was the attitude I was encouraged to take and, as much as possible, that was the attitude my parents took towards me.

I have no legs. To me, in many ways, this is a deficiency in the same way that a bald man has no hair. I spent my childhood in a normal family, having good fun, getting a belting when I deserved one, doing the things that little boys do when they are growing up. I didn't see myself as being much different from everybody else. Sure, I knew they were doing physically active things that I would have loved to have been doing, such as playing Rugby League and soccer and outdoor cricket. I yearned for the ability to pedal a bike. But there were things I did that my brothers and friends couldn't do, such as playing wheelchair League, so in my mind we were just about even.

My parents hammered the point that I wasn't to be left out of things, or be let off when blame was being apportioned if I was the villain. Yes, although I am a little bit different and a lot shorter than my brothers and sister, we kids were all treated the same. If there were things near the top of the cupboard and there was someone there to help, then help I got, but if I was there on my own then I worked out a way to reach it. And once I'd worked out how to do it, I didn't need help to get up to that top shelf again. Almost always, there was a way to get to that top shelf.

Evelyn Coutis: I only helped John with things he couldn't reach. We never ever adjusted the house to suit him; he had to adjust. I never considered that there was anything wrong with him, except that he couldn't walk.

I was raised by my parents to see myself as somebody a little bit different rather than simply as a 'disabled' person. Sure, I had this awful deformity thing with my legs but I wasn't different from my elder brother, my younger brother, my sister or my cousins. For me to call myself disabled was not the done thing. Consequently today I don't see myself as being limited in any way. I see myself as someone who is physically different from everybody else and someone who has had to confront different challenges from those most people face. These challenges have made me work harder, driven me harder. They have also maximised the desire in my heart to do all the things I really want to do.

Sometimes, in a quiet moment, I think back to when it all began. My life could have evolved in any number of ways. If I'd been pampered or treated like a lesser being, I might not have been able to look after myself later on, not been able to feed myself or even go to the toilet by myself. I've been to homes for the disabled and seen kids and young adults who began their lives in a similar state to how I found myself. They, I learnt, had started off as mobile and agile as I had been, but whereas their situation deteriorated, mine improved. How lucky was I to have parents as strong as my Mum and Dad? I'm just so grateful that they gave me an opportunity to really live life. They gave me a start, a huge, enormous, gigantic start.

Liberty Coutis: One day he did something to his father, I forget what it was, and Gary put him out in the front yard. He was screaming to come in but Gary said to me, 'Don't go and get him. Leave him there; he's gotta learn.' So I had to leave him there while he was screaming. No, John didn't get any privileges because he had no legs. He got hidings, he got everything, whatever was there. He did it wrong, he got punished.

Mum and Dad had no end of people telling them that you couldn't do this and you shouldn't do that. One infamous story concerns the day that Dad took me out the backyard with our dog, Candy, and left me there. I was screaming and howling and howling and screaming, to the point that the phone started ringing. It was the next-door neighbours, then the bloke two houses down, then the woman three houses down, calling to express their concern.

'Gary, do you know your son's in your backyard with your dog, and he's bawling his eyes out?'

'Gary, shouldn't you see if he's okay?'

'Gary, what's the matter with him?'

'You sure you know what you're doin', Gary?'

'Yeah, I do,' my Dad calmly replied to each of them. 'Leave him alone. It'll be all right.'

What had happened was that Dad had had enough of the fact that I was scared of the dog. It wasn't that I didn't like the animal – in fact, I used to love playing with her and teasing her, so long as there was a screen door between her and me. But if she was in the same room, with nothing but fresh air separating us, I went to pieces. Dad got sick of telling me that she wasn't going to hurt me. So he took me out into the backyard with her, and left us to it.

Finally my crying did stop – after about three or four hours. When Dad came out to check on me I was sitting on Candy's back, throwing mock punches at her, riding her around the yard. Dad knew me and he knew Candy. I wasn't in danger, just terrified, which I needed to get over. It was a tough but effective way to learn.

I used to love hosing my fellow kids with water but hated being hosed myself, to the point that I'd be only too happy to dob in any wet bugger who turned the hose on me. Dad taught me a lesson one day when he wised up to this scam. Before I could turn the hose on anyone, he grabbed it off me and turned the tap up full volume. I nearly drowned! Later, he explained why I deserved it, but in a funny kind of way I already knew.

There's nothing I can do about having no legs and there's nothing I can do about any of my other disabilities. I have no legs, and that's it. I'm ugly and I've got a terrible sense of humour, too, but – despite the constant complaints of my wife – I can't do anything about those, either.

Even if, by some miracle, I could get some legs and was able to walk, I don't think I would. In fact, I know I wouldn't. What I am is what I am. I have lived the last 30-plus years of my life like this. They say a change is as good as a holiday, but is it really? I'm perfectly happy as is, thank you very much. Deep down inside, I really like myself. Sure, there are times when I don't feel *that* good about me, but I have committed myself to getting past those off days. I won't let them consume me.

I'm the first to admit that there have been moments when I was younger when I *did* want to change things. On one occasion that I'll deal with in detail on later pages, I even wanted to end things. But whenever I felt sorry for myself, I remembered my parents' advice: *Life isn't perfect but it isn't all bad. Smell the roses.*

Back then, I was desperate to be the same as everybody else. But what is the same these days? For a while, my dream was to be able-bodied. Eventually, I wanted to have no legs and be disabled. At times, I even wished I could have the best of both worlds. Nowadays I consider myself very lucky. I am proud of who I am and keen to stand up for what I believe in. You can do that, you know, even if you have no legs.

This is my life, not anybody else's. To my mind, if I was to suddenly get some legs, whether through a miracle of medicine or artificial technology, I'd become something of a phoney. Times have changed. I'm older and wiser and I don't want to be a fake. What I want to be is the best person I can be every single day, and for me that means living without legs and dealing with it. It certainly doesn't mean sitting here feeling sorry for myself. It's time to get on with life.

Of course I am not the only person without legs who has made something of his or her life. There are many others who have succeeded, often in vastly different ways from me. The common thread is that we have all tried, had a go. Still, a lot of people are amazed that I do many of the things I do and have the zest for life that I do, but to me that's just a result of deciding to try to make the most out of what I've been dealt. So many people are stunned that I can drive a car. The fact that I can get up and down a staircase quicker than they can is a further source of amazement for them and pride for me. But if I hadn't made myself do these things, nowadays I wouldn't even be able to get off my chair. It's the way that Mum and Dad raised me.

In my first three decades I've seen the world slowly adapt to all kinds of different people from all walks of life, different races, different attitudes, different agendas, different colours, different physical abilities, different mental abilities. While I know there is still much more to do, the changes that have occurred are quite astounding. This is also a reflection on just how 'backward' we were as a society in the 1960s, but as far as my situation goes, I'm just thankful I was born when I was. If I'd arrived a few years earlier, I'd have been shoved in a home for sure, probably never to escape.

My physical disability has meant that there are a number of things I can't do, and a number of things that I can't do 'normally', but if ever I wanted something badly enough then I found a way to do it or get it. If I didn't do it or get it, then it probably wasn't really that important. That's something I've found time and again throughout my life: if you don't desire something too badly then you shouldn't worry about the barriers preventing you from getting it. That 'something' can't be too important to you. Move on to things that are.

Most of my biggest challenges came when I was young. That was when the struggles to get over my hurdles were most difficult and most infuriating. Simple things. Being able to sit on a chair – it took ages to learn how to do that. Being able to climb onto a table or go up a ladder, even go to the toilet. Throughout I needed people to guide me and love me. I hesitate to say 'help' me because that implies that I couldn't do anything for myself. But I did need a lot of support and fortunately I received it.

This need for love and encouragement applies to us all. Everyone needs support to overcome their own limitations, whatever those limitations might be. The key is to find those people who will give you love; without them you're lost. My guardian angels were my parents, who were always strong and taught me so much. I've always believed one of the main reasons my Mum was put on this earth was to look after me. My partners in crime were my two brothers and my sister.

Let me introduce them to you.

Family
Matters

I HAVE SUCH A loving family. This said, during my life I've still had my share of barneys with my brothers and my sister, and with my Mum and Dad.

The day I turned 16 I thought I was suddenly big enough to take on my father. I wasn't. I've never been big enough to take on my father. He's a huge bloke who I love to death. Dad's parents were Greek, a couple who came to Australia independently of each other when they were children. Their union was the result of one of those marital arrangements that used to happen in Greek society, and although there was a lot of love in their relationship, there was a lot of differences, too. There were 17 years difference between the ages of my Pop and my Nan. Pop was a mad gambler who'd bet on two flies going up a wall, which didn't sit at all well with Nan. One day, she told me, Pop disappeared for a weekend. No one knew where he was or what he might have done. He was lost, AWOL, MIA, gone. Eventually he did return, with just a ragged old singlet on his back. Lost everything. The story goes that at one point my Pop had enough money to own all of Richmond; at other times things weren't quite that flash.

If he'd worked on his wealth, things could have been different for future Coutis generations. But we never think about that; it's in the past, no one can change it. One thing I do know is that Nan was a real soldier to put up with such stuff, and with the antics of my father, my uncle and my Auntie Katrina. My grandparents also had twins, but sadly they died not long after their birth. Such tragedies were a part of life back in those days; fortunately, modern medicine gives many more kids the chance to show how tough they can be.

The earliest memories I have of my Old Man are of a big burly bloke who could make young kids tremble in their shoes as soon as they heard his deep, powerful voice. He's a carpenter by trade and a Rugby League coach, too – good enough to coach the A-grade team at Colo in the Penrith district for 11 years. In that time, his sides reached something like seven grand finals and won four of them. During his tenure at Colo he coached my elder brother,

Adam, and my younger brother, Luke, but for all three of us, and for my sister, Kristy, he was much more than just a coach. He has always been a great father and our best friend.

There's no doubt that Dad won a lot of respect in the community because of his involvement in the footy club. Not only was he a long-time coach, he was also president for a while, and secretary and treasurer. In 1975, Dad put his tools in the back of the shed and opened a food shop, 'Gazza's Northo Take-Away'. His menu quickly became the talk of the surrounding districts, and it was nothing for people to drive from half an hour, even an hour away, to pick up a roast chicken or a couple of hamburgers and then sit by the Nepean River and eat them.

Many of my childhood memories evolved from that shop. Little things, such as Dad grabbing a carton of strawberry milk from the fridge at the front of the shop and hurling it at one of my brothers as he scampered out the back. I can still see that carton smashing into the back wall and its contents dripping down the paintwork. I remember, too, my Old Man repeating to us, whenever we decided that dinner wasn't to our liking, 'If you don't eat it, you're gonna wear it; you don't eat it, you're gonna wear it.' We ate it. You've heard the old saying, 'You are what you eat.' Well, we learnt that if you don't eat it, you're that as well. We had custard tarts tipped on our heads, and spaghetti sandwiches and tuna sandwiches and meat pies. When we were growing up, our father was a man of his word. Still is. If you don't eat it, you're gonna wear it.

I said Dad won plenty of admiration from the local community for his big contribution to the footy club. I reckon he also earnt a lot of respect for the way he raised his family. For being a leader, backing his judgment, not caring what others thought. Mum and Dad copped a lot of shit from so many people who thought *they* knew best. 'He has to go into a home,' these often well-meaning people would say. 'He needs special care, which you can't give.' But Mum and Dad could give me care that no one else could offer and they were brave enough and smart enough and loving enough to recognise this. Dad jumped up, waved the knockers away and said, 'The only home he's going into is ours.'

Home is where I went and home is where I stayed, to be raised with a lot of love and a lot of care and, I've got to tell you, a hell of a lot of discipline, too. But, you know, that discipline really helped me, as it helped my brothers and sister. Dad remains a staunch believer in the value of impressing standards upon your children. Never forget – there's a huge difference between disciplining your child and belting the hell out of them. It's called caring. I know we never copped a disciplining that we didn't deserve, and I also know that we never copped a disciplining that didn't teach us the difference between right and wrong. This said, I must confess that I was something of a prick when I was a kid. I set the cat on fire half a dozen times, and it wasn't even our cat.

Dad never disciplined us in front of anybody else – unless we were extremely wicked! – but he was a champion at saving things up for when we got home. Personally I'd have rather he did get us there and then, because the physical pain we suffered was always greater after he'd been stewing on our latest screw up.

More often than not, Dad would say, 'Choose your weapon.' This meant 'Put your hand out, don't move it, if you move it, you're going to get six more, hold it up there, don't you start crying, I'll give you something to cry about.' Whack! It used to bloody hurt; it never tickled. In a way, I was lucky. Because of the way I walked, my hands were a bit tougher than everybody else's.

Whatever you think of this form of punishment, it taught us a lot. So much of what Mum and Dad did for us knocked us into shape, educated us about the ways of this world. These were things you can't always learn in school, doing a trade, studying at university or at college. Values. Respect your country, be proud of your heritage, love your family, respect the law, have fun, enjoy life, be proud of who you are, don't ever give up, believe in yourself. Stand tall. Mum and Dad taught me how to stand tall, for which I will always be grateful.

My Dad, supported 100 per cent by his devoted wife, built a loving family with his bare hands. Ours was a life full of values, warmth and good times. Sure, there were some bad times thrown in, but thank God there were because otherwise we'd have taken all the good ones for granted.

My Mum's hands are the moulding hands, the holding hands, the nurturing hands. I used to come home from school and there she was to give me a big hug. She'd pull me towards her and suddenly everything would be okay. 'I love you, John,' she'd remind me. As if I needed reminding, but I never stopped her, and never shied away from that love. 'You are the best thing that's happened in our lives,' she'd tell me. 'You're a good person.' That's my mother – so warm, so caring. We had our arguments and fights and all of that, too, but when I look back on it even the blues were worthwhile. Mum did many things her neighbours said she shouldn't as she gave me the opportunity to grow as a person. She cracked a few wooden spoons over my head, as well, but that was only because my butt was too close to the ground and she couldn't reach it!

It's funny, you know. While I have certainly developed my own personality and my own character as I've grown older, I now find myself approaching situations the same way my Dad used to. Similarly, I sometimes find myself saying things that Mum would say. I've definitely inherited certain traits from my parents. This said, I'd still like to think that I'm my own person and that I judge others' characters for myself. I really drive myself hard to truly get out of life what I want. That comes from within.

In the days when I was a young fella, North Richmond was a small country town. Today it's a genuine suburb on the north-western outskirts of the Sydney metropolitan area, but back in the 1970s it was just a little dot far from the big city. The most significant thing at Richmond was the RAAF base, which dominated the landscape and the skies while employing many of the district's men and women. A fair percentage of the houses in North Richmond were either Department of Housing or Defence Force dwellings.

We moved there in early 1970, when I was five months old, to a house at 69 Grose Vale Road. Sixty-nine – the year I was born, the number of my Mum and Dad's house, the name of my indoor cricket side. It was a three-bedroom, brick-veneer place on a fair sized block of land. Originally our property had been part of a dairy farm, then it was sub-divided. As Dad made a few bucks, he pulled down the garage and put a pool in. Then came some extra rooms out the back, then some more up through the ceiling, and finally a brand new garage. That little three-bedroom house was transformed into a seven-bedroom, four-bathroom, double-garaged home with a pool. We kids just sat there and watched it grow. Like anything, you feed it well and look after it, then it'll take care of you. Dad did an absolutely fantastic job building our home.

To develop that home, Mum and Dad both worked hard – no more so than a lot of other mums and dads, I know, but bloody hard all the same. This meant that when Mum was working nights and Dad was at the shop, we were at the shop as well. But this was okay, because if it was sweltering – as summer nights often were – we could spend some time in the cool room. And if it wasn't so hot or humid there were living quarters out the back of the shop where many a night was spent doing homework, watching television or eating dinner. We even set up a slot-car track out there, where many a Grand Prix was won or lost. One other thing I remember about that room out the back of the shop was the fridge – during a game of hide'n'seek, I climbed inside and shut the door, which proved to be an excellent move, at least in terms of the game. Only trouble was, the hiding place was so good no one could find me, and I couldn't open the door. By the time I was finally rescued, by someone innocently looking for a cool drink, I was terrified.

Our most regular 'babysitter' was our grandmother, Nan (Liberty is her name but to us she is Nan), a wonderful woman. She used to do everything she could for us. Nan had come out to Australia from Greece when she was just two years old, in 1923, to live first in The Rocks, not far from the ships at Circular Quay, then in the St George district in the southern suburbs, and then out to Richmond.

Liberty Coutis: I used to mind them because Eve had to work. I'd go up there in the morning and mind them. I went up this particular day, and there were stairs out the back, about 12 or 14 steps. 'Nan, I want to go downstairs.' I'd take him down the stairs. 'Nan, I want to go upstairs.' I'd take him up the stairs. 'Nan, I want to go downstairs.' He just kept going, so I said to him, 'John, you either stay downstairs or you come up the stairs. I'm not taking you up or down all the time.' So he finally stopped downstairs and he said to me, 'Think about these poor little legs, Nan.'

Those poor little legs!

The lunches Nan made for us to take to school were special. She would pack them into these little blue eskies, which had a frozen block inside the lid to keep everything cold. At times, we'd exploit our Nan's efforts by taking some of our lunches, and other stock we'd pinched from the back of the store, and flogging them on the black market at school.

The most popular things we sold were my Nan's Greek biscuits. We used to make a pretty packet out of them, just quietly. Best of all were the shortbread biscuits with the white icing, which also provided a bit of a laugh for us when they were bought by unsuspecting kids who didn't know how to eat them. Swallow 'em too fast and the icing would get caught in your throat, which led to a number of near-deaths in the playground from choking. They just had absolutely no idea.

More than merely minding us, our grandmother taught us a lot. One Christmas she caught my cousin Peter and me swearing in Greek. We, naively, had assumed that if those around us didn't understand what we were saying then we weren't breaking any rules. Nan set us straight, and then reminded the pair of us how important it was to learn from our mistakes.

I love my Nan and used to go with her on some of her appointments. One day she was in a doctor's consulting room while I was in the waiting room. As I flicked through an edition of *Reader's Digest*, the room began to fill with other patients, many of whom, I couldn't help but notice, were looking at me with raised eyebrows. Finally my Nan finished her appointment and we headed for the exit, none too soon in my book. It was then, as we walked out into the sunlight, that I saw the doctor's office sign. That's why I'd been getting funny looks. Nan had just been to the podiatrist.

When I introduced myself to the world so traumatically in 1969 there was already one boy in the Coutis family. Adam is two years older than me. One thing I learnt from him was that not everybody excels at the same thing. Early on I thought Adam was a genius at everything, but then along came younger brother Luke, who showed me that there were plenty of things that he could do even better than Adam. And Adam also demonstrated how there were many things Luke wasn't that flash at. The one constant between the three of us was that we were all extremely competitive. I was, and remain, incredibly proud of them, but I also have to admit that when I was a kid I envied them. I wanted to be in their shoes, doing the things they were doing, even though I knew that such a miracle was never going to happen. I worked out very slowly that I could never do things their way. I had to do them my way.

I was on the sidelines as Adam graduated through the football club's ranks. I saw him get his driver's licence. I watched him do so many things that I wanted to do. And, you know, gradually I took the attitude that if he could do it, so could I. In my own way, eventually I did.

Evelyn Coutis: Adam wasn't aggressive, he was more passive and would walk away from a fight. But Luke was different. I remember he once jumped up and belted a Year 12 kid when he was little, because that kid was picking on John. Luke was only in Year 8. He was a skinny little fella then, too, but he jumped up and punched this Year 12 kid.

Luke and I were always getting each other into trouble. Some of the schemes and tricks and accidents waiting to happen that we perpetrated were, looking back, truly awful, and, looking back with a chuckle, bloody funny. One day Adam was asleep and – I don't know what possessed us to do this, we just did it – we grabbed a little spud (as in potato) gun, armed it with a spud, and tiptoed into his bedroom. There was big brother, snoring happily away. I was nine, maybe ten, Luke was eight, maybe seven, so Adam was 11, could have been 12. I looked at Luke, looked at Adam, Luke looked at me; we can't do this – but we did.

Luke and I exchanged glances again. This, we decided with a quiet giggle, is going to be great! We pulled the trigger. Boom! Straight and a long way into Adam's ear. And then he's no longer snoring, he's hitting the roof. Literally. Mum! Mum! Luke and I, scoundrels that we were (and still are!), were rolling around on the floor, laughing our heads off. Adam ran out of his room. 'Mum! What have they done?' It took Mum three-and-a-half hours, with a bobby pin and a safety pin, to get that potato out of Adam's ear. Afterwards there was hell to pay for Luke and Johnno Coutis. The punishment fitted the crime and it hurt for a while, but at the time we felt it was worth it. Geez, he jumped a long way! Like I said, I was often something of a prick when I was young.

> **Gary Coutis:** We used to go down the beach and we'd take John out. His brothers used to drag him out and put him on a wave and send him back in again and then come and get him. John'd be shouting, 'Do it again! Do it again!'

Adam could also be our partner in crime. On one weekend he made a billycart out of my sister's pram. Kristy no longer needed the pram to get around, but Mum was using it to store all Kristy's dolls and toys and stuff. However, we thought it was okay to hijack it; after all, there were other things, such as a cupboard or a washing basket, that could have served as a toy box, but as we quickly learnt there is no better frame for a billycart than a pram. That pram was exactly what we needed, so we snaffled it, and Adam went to work.

Luke's contribution to this escapade was to find one of Mum's best white towels and paint black checks all over it with a fat texta so it looked like a chequered flag. He'd also found an old stopwatch of Dad's, so he could time all the track records.

On this famous day, I was watching out the front window as Adam proudly dragged his new cart up to the top of our street while Luke waited outside our house to wave him home. The street led up a steep hill, perfect for what we had in mind. Before Adam jumped into the driver's seat he donned his helmet – an old ice-cream container,

complete with eyes painted on the top to keep the mag-
pies at bay and tied tight under the chin by a dirty old
shoelace.

Adam hopped in, straightened his helmet, tightened the
shoelace one more time, and then he was off. Luke waited,
flag in hand. Woooosh! Through the glass I could hear his
screams of glee, and feel the joy in his heart as the wind
blew his helmet off. Luke waved him home, using that chequered towel (sorry Mum!) with a great flourish.

Then it was Luke's turn. The helmet was way too big,
but who cared? Adam was there with that towel to welcome him across the line. At the time, back in the house,
my heart was saying, 'Go on, go for it.' My head was
yelling, 'Don't be an idiot, you'll hurt yourself.'

Each took it in turn to have the ride of their lives. Eventually I could stand it no longer, so I ran out and cried, 'I
wanna go, I wanna go, I wanna go!

'Yagottalemme'aveago!'

Adam, big brother, straightaway said, 'No, no, no, it's
too dangerous. You'll hurt yourself for sure.'

'C'mon, gimme a go.'

Luke was on my side. 'Yeah, go on,' he grinned. 'Give
'im a go, it'll be cool.'

'What'll Dad say?' Adam cautioned.

Then I started crying, which I knew would get him.
And, of course, it did. 'Bloody hell, you little bastard. In
you go.'

He jumped out, threw me in, and then dragged the billycart back up the hill. Luke waited down the bottom,

chequered towel in hand. Up the top of that incline – Christ, it's a bit steep, I suddenly realised – Adam strapped on the helmet. Then he quickly told me how to steer. Pull it this way to go left, this way for right. And then he set me on my way.

It was so *unbelievably good*! The most enormous adrenalin rush I'd ever had by a million miles. The kind of thing little boys dream of and the kind of thing I had been dreaming of for years. If I pulled the steering rope this way, I went that way, pull it that way I went this way. I was all over the shop, as if I was wrestling a big crocodile, but I was eight years old and having the time of my life. Finally, in no time at all, I reached the finish line. Luke waved that chequered towel even more extravagantly than ever. And then it hit me.

'Hey, Luke, how do I stop this *bloody thing*!'

And Luke yelled back, 'Throw your legs out!'

'My God,' I screamed inside. 'What am I going to do?' The billycart was now a bucking bronco. About another 600 metres down the road, after a terrifying, exhilarating, awful, thrilling ride, I finally came to a halt. First I crashed into the gutter, then the billycart and I rolled across the footpath and ended up in someone's rosebush. When my brothers reached me – presuming I was dead as they ran, and rehearsing explanations and excuses for the Old Man – I was stuck between two very thorny branches, frightened, bleeding and deliriously happy, with a big, black dog nonchalantly licking my face.

Adam harried the dog away, and then the three of us sat there, me still wedged in the rosebush branches. We were laughing and laughing and laughing. And in between the laughter Adam was saying, 'God, look at you, bleeding from nine holes. Dad's gonna kill me.'

'Why don't we give 'im another go?' Luke suggested.

I felt like such a grown-up!

Gavin Robertson (Australian cricketer, drummer with the band Six and Out, and family friend): You walk into the Coutis home today and you learn that all that stuff he talks about is not bullshit, it's just the way it is.

John said to me once, 'I love *The Simpsons*.'

I replied, 'Why? I'm not a big fan.'

He said, 'Oh, it's just a classic dysfunctional family like all of us.'

And, you know, there's a heap of families out there who think they're perfect. I reckon we are all a bit dysfunctional in a way, but I just hope I can bring my kids up to be in a dysfunctional family like the Coutises.

As I've said, Luke was my partner in prank after prank. I was Merlin the magician and he was my faithful assistant, which was a bit silly really because I should have been the one in the box being sawn in half. We were always in trouble together. If I did something wrong, we both got a flogging. He became my best mate as I was growing up, an absolute champion.

As we got older we developed an entrepreneurial streak. One day Adam had a brilliant idea. 'Let's set up a stall out the front and sell the Old Man's spare nails.' Dad had so many in his shed, we were sure he wouldn't miss a few, so we put them into little bags and offered them for sale. Then we found some of Dad's rope and thought we'd try to sell some of that, cut into two-foot lengths. Business was brisk, and we soon found that we had a black market for all Dad's nails, all Dad's rope, and some of Dad's best tools as well.

And then Adam saw Dad driving up the road, coming home earlier than usual. Uh, oh. Big brother bolted, did the runner, so Luke and I were left to shovel all our stock into a bag and scamper for the backyard and from there under the house, where we hoped Dad wouldn't find us or our loot. Of course hiding under the house was a good idea because there was little chance of the Old Man looking there, but not so smart because we had no means of escape. We didn't dare try to sneak out while Dad might be looking out the back windows. While Dad was home, we were stuck.

We heard him park the car in the driveway and then walk to the back door. Under the house, as the day headed towards night, it eventually became pitch black; we couldn't even see the whites of our eyes. Every time either of us suggested in hushed tones that now was a good time to make our escape, the other said no way, better to wait and hope the old bloke went out. Then it started to get cold. On the ground we could feel nails that had fallen out of their bags, and rope and hammers and other tools. Then Luke stumbled upon what he thought was a box of matches. He struck a match and we had some light. Nearby were some paper plates and some timber. Plenty of fuel. As we started to shiver, I had the brilliant idea to light a fire. We were only young, remember. Within minutes we'd built a roaring bonfire, which would have been fantastic – if we'd been out in the backyard.

Today I can still picture Mum sniffing the air and saying to Dad, 'Gary, do you smell smoke?' As we kept throwing things on our fire, the flames were jumping a couple of metres high, which would have been great except that under the house the floorboards were only about 30 centimetres above my head. One minute, the fire was brilliant, then things started to get a little out of control.

The next thing you know, bang! The door under the house sprung open and there was Dad, looking absolute daggers at us. We had a saying in those days, whenever we knew Dad was going to blow a fuse, 'Uh, oh. There's gonna be a gunfight.' He dragged us out by the hair, threw us on the ground, and then grabbed the hose and put the fire out. We didn't move a muscle; we were shivering, quivering and as black as any ace of spades from all the dirt and smoke. When Dad had finally calmed everything down except himself, he took us inside and bounced us off every wall as he drove home the point that what we'd done was bloody stupid. Throughout all that carnage, there was Adam watching in the distance. He could be a little bastard, my big brother.

We learnt a lesson that day but we weren't totally reformed. Just a fraction smarter. Our speciality became the practical joke, with emphasis on the 'practical', usually played on family members but sometimes on the public at large. Our favourite was what we called 'The Wallet', which used to work an absolute treat because we lived on a main road and had four beautiful big pine trees guarding the front of the house.

We used to sit in the dirt and the leaves and the pine needles underneath one of those trees, camouflaged, and wait as cars and bikes and trucks drove past. The scheme was to tie one of Dad's old wallets to a fishing line, and cast it out into the middle of the road. And then a car or truck or ute would come along.

Screeeeech!

Sooner or later a vehicle would pull up, having seen what they must have thought was some lazy money lying on the road. The only trouble was that even while the brakes were still screaming we were madly winding the wallet back in. So when the driver ran over to where they'd seen it, there was nothing for them to pick up. Early on, just seeing these blokes looking around and then shaking their heads as they returned to their vehicle was good enough for us. But, ever gradually, we got bolder and bolder, and wouldn't wind the wallet back until the driver was well and truly out of the car. More than once we had blokes running towards our front yard, chasing the wallet as it scampered back under the tree.

Eventually we came unstuck. One driver saw the wallet and pulled up with his tyres slapbang on the fishing line. The wallet wouldn't come back to us. The driver calmly picked it up, jumped back in his car, and threw the wallet onto his passenger seat. He'd wait till later to see if there was any cash inside. The biggest problem from our point of view was that he hadn't noticed the wallet was attached to some fishing line. So when he took off, he took the line with him which created a major problem for a moment because Luke, like a fisherman determined not to let go of the biggest catch of his life, refused to let go even though the car was clearly too big to be hauled in. Fortunately, the line snapped, but it could have got messy.

Before that we'd had one young bloke on a bike ride all the way into the pine trees chasing the wallet. Luckily, he wasn't dirty on us. Instead, he thought it was a great lark and stayed with us for a while as we had some fun with a few more disgruntled motorists.

Gary Coutis: I came home one day and my HQ two-door Monaro was sitting in the drive. It was what Mum used to drive. John and his brothers had the hose in the window of the car filling it up. I yelled, 'What are you doin'?'

'We're fillin' her up, Dad, and givin' her a wash.'

Shit!

Their mother had had a bad day and had just conked out inside. I think she knew that I wouldn't be far away. And the kids decided to go and fill the car up, to wash it. I had to open the bloody door and let the water out. I got me hammer out and had to punch some holes through the floor to let it all out.

Luke developed into an excellent sportsman, a good enough Rugby League player, in my biased view, to play rep footy, if that's what he'd wanted. One of the things entrenched in my memory is the way we used to get around together, the way we used to go to his footy together. Luke owned an old trusty mountain bike; I had my just-as-trusty skateboard. If we were in a hurry or had a fair distance to travel, we'd use one of Dad's old ropes to connect the two – tied to the back of the bike at one end and clasped firmly by my hands at the other. And then Luke would set off, dragging me sitting on my board. Early on this meant I spent some time introducing myself head-first to the bitumen, but as I got the hang of it we were able to build up a reasonable speed, and then as I got cockier the rope we used got longer and longer.

After Dad closed the take-away in 1981, he went back to his carpentry trade, working for a company that specialised in building kitchens. One time, Luke and I were hanging around at Dad's factory, so to give us something worthwhile to do he sent us to the local hardware store to get something – I can't remember exactly what – that he needed in a hurry. Actually he asked *me* to go, but I quickly pointed out that I would have trouble carrying whatever it was back, so then he said, a bit reluctantly (he knew what scoundrels we were), 'Orright, take Luke with you.'

The sensible thing would have been to go at a nice steady pace, but Dad did say he needed it in a hurry. So we got the old rope out and tied it to the bike; I clambered on my skateboard; Luke jumped on his bike; I grabbed hold, and off we sped. From there to the store and back, all we could hear were the sounds of car horns beeping and blasting, and angry and astonished drivers yelling out all sorts of expletives at us and at life. I just held on for all I was worth, swapped swearwords with the real drivers, and roared and roared with laughter.

In no time we were back at the factory. In the driveway was a huge pile of sand. Skateboards don't go real good in sand, but Luke wasn't worried about that as he weaved past. For me there was no escape and, like a waterskier being slingshot over a jump, I crashed straight in and then over. The skateboard stopped as if it was stuck in glue, but I kept going, too scared and excited to let go. Luke, eyes only for the next hazard ahead, presumed everything behind was okay; after all, the weight felt pretty much the same. Maybe he should have noticed that what he was towing was now bouncing all over the place and banging into anything and everything. Why I didn't just let go, I don't know, but nothing in my life had prepared me for this experience. All I know is that fear took hold at exactly the same time as logic went out the window. By the time we finally stopped, I had no shirt left on my front, a big graze up my chest, a chin and nose that were missing way too much skin, and teeth that were now razor sharp from all the concrete I'd chewed. All because I wouldn't let go of that bloody rope.

After Luke there is my sister Kristy. She was an absolutely beautiful child. Remember the old Arnott's chocolate 'golliwog' biscuits? That was her – dark, olive skin from her Greek heritage and frizzy hair to complete the picture. Growing up with three older brothers inevitably meant there was a bit of tomboy in her, to the point that she even played Rugby League when she was seven or eight years old. And what a player! She was tough, too; I worked out real quick not to pick a fight with her.

Yet as a kid she wouldn't wear a battle wound. When I ripped my body to bits being dragged back from the hardware store, the thing I hated most was going back to Mum. She was a nurse by profession, and she used to tell us that we should suffer through our war wounds, that she had genuinely sick people to treat at work so why should she have to deal with self-inflicted wounds when she got home. Sure, Mum patched us up, but she wanted us to be tough and sensible, so we became acutely embarrassed on the rare occasions when we needed her professional care.

Kristy was different. A mummy's girl whenever she got hurt. One day my faithful assistant Luke and I were in Kristy's bedroom, having decided that the room would be more useful if it was remodelled as a circus tent. First we took the mattress off her bed and lay it down beside the wardrobe. Then Luke climbed up into the top compartment of the wardrobe and dived out, completing a series of manoeuvres with varying degrees of difficulty before landing safely on the mattress. Initially Kristy was happy to watch but gradually she thought, 'Hey, this looks cool,' and then, egged on by Luke, she climbed up to have a go herself. I was the big brother back on ground level. 'Are you sure this is okay, John?' she asked.

'Absolutely!'

So she climbed up and into the top compartment, twisted her little body around, gazed out, then down at the little mattress on the floorboards. Then – one, two, three – she burst out of the wardrobe and dropped like a stone, missing the mattress but hitting her head on the steel post of the bed. Straightaway she was howling. 'Mum! Mum! *Mum*!'

Uh, oh. There's gonna be a gunfight.

I tried giving her a hug, saying, 'Shhhh, shhhh. Everything'll be okay.' Kristy, of course, was howling. 'Shhhh, shhhh. Don't worry, stop crying. Stop crying; it didn't hurt.'

We were going to be in so much trouble. Or maybe not. Kristy started to quieten down. In fact, we almost had her. But do you remember how when you were a kid that if you saw blood then somehow a bump or a cut suddenly hurt way more than it had a second before? You really were going to die. Well Kristy looked down at the fingers that had been holding her head and saw blood and immediately started screaming so loud it made her previous cries seem like tame whimpers. Oh, mate, were we in trouble. She needed three stitches in the middle of her forehead, and after Dad was finished with Luke and me, our hands felt as if they needed stitching back up as well.

My little sister was always wanting to do everything that the boys were doing. At one point, Adam and Luke created a bike track around the front yard, on which they staged races with a few of their mates. Within minutes our little sister wanted to be involved. This time, having learnt from past mistakes, we consulted Dad, who said it was okay. So Kristy hopped on a bike, completed one or two laps but then, you wouldn't believe it, she stacked it. From my vantage point, it seemed as if she tried to ride the bike straight up a tree. If she'd stayed on the track, she explained to me later, there was no way she was going to win.

A few years earlier, Adam and Luke had tried to teach her how to ride a bike. It was simple really. We lived on a big block that backed onto some vacant land. And on that vacant land was a decent hill, from which my brothers sometimes charged down and into the backyard. One day they took Kristy to the top of the hill, sat her on the bike and showed her how to steer. The fact that she couldn't reach the pedals wasn't a concern because the trip was to be all downhill. And then they let her go, the plan being that they'd run alongside to make sure nothing went wrong. Unfortunately, they underestimated how much speed she could build up, and within seconds she was away, the wind blowing through her hair, her shrieks of joy ringing through the air. And then she started to head off track, directly towards a wooden fence, and all we could do was watch. What happened next was a miracle.

Sure enough, the bike collided into the fence, with Kristy going at a fair speed. But instead of being flung over the handlebars, little sister managed to hang on. The bike's front wheel stayed wedged between two fence palings, so tight that the bike remained upright. Kristy just sat on it, white knuckles wrapped around the handles, transfixed on the seat. Luke and Adam, having dashed to her side, now fell back laughing. I was still at the top of the hill, taking it all in. It was quite a sight.

Soon we were all laughing, even Kristy. Eventually we even told Mum and Dad. They said we were bloody idiots but they laughed, too. We laughed a lot in those good ol' days back at North Richmond.

They were happy times.

I imagine, as you read my stories about our childhood pranks, you're thinking, So what's so special? There were plenty of pranks in my life when I was growing up. Exactly. My point is that I was lucky – given the physical constraints nature had thrown at me – to have the chance to do these things. I was lucky my parents gave me that chance. I was lucky my brothers and sister gave me that chance. I was lucky they treated me like a 'normal' child. I was lucky I was part of a loving family, lucky to be taught some valuable lessons about life, to be disciplined when I deserved it, to be hugged when I needed it, to be cared about every minute of every day.

Joe Hutton (John's friend and 'minder' on speaking tours):
What I like about John is his strong belief and faith in family. Whenever we tour, he rings his Mum, Dad, sister, brothers – he's always talking about family.

One thing that became obvious very quickly was that North Richmond was not really made for kids in wheelchairs. Back in those days it wasn't suitable for anyone with a so-called 'disability'. Like many people's minds, the roads were dirt. Of course my experiences growing up were very different from those of a 'normal' child. Because my legs were useless I was restricted in what I could physically do, and what activities I could enjoy, but more than that, my unusual appearance meant that most people didn't know how to take me. It's not that people who didn't know me deliberately ostracised me, but their inability to treat me as they would a 'normal' person meant I often felt ostracised. Dad used to compare the way people treated me with how he and his family were treated back before I was born, back when if you weren't of good British stock in Australia then you were a 'wog'. And if you were a wog then there was always a chance you'd get insulted or even belted simply because you were a wog. The people who were doing the insulting or the belting just didn't understand. All Dad could do was live with it, but that didn't mean he had to enjoy it.

Mum and Dad taught me not to worry about what people say. 'Learn to be ignorant,' they wisely advised. 'Don't worry about what people do when they stare or mistreat you.'

I used to reckon I was pretty good with a pencil and paper – still do! One day I was sitting in my wheelchair, out in front of my Dad's take-away food shop, doing some drawings, and I decided to try to flog my best work, just to earn a little pocket money. Many passers-by were very kind, and I made the odd buck or two, but less encouraging were the sniggers and stares and pointing and giggles from unknowing children. Also desperately offputting were the parents who could do no more than drag their offspring away by the ear, or give them a gentle prod to try to get their kids to move on. I guess these children were inquisitive rather than malicious, but it wasn't good for me, especially the way both children *and* parents would turn around, about 10 or 15 metres down the road, and have one more long look.

Years later I read a book by the actor Whoopi Goldberg, in which she responded to the question, 'Does it bother you what people call you?' I know it used to hurt me, it really did. Whoopi's answer was, 'It doesn't matter what people call you; what matters is what you answer to.'

I see a lot of value in such a philosophy. It comes back to having pride in yourself, or not having pride in yourself. It doesn't matter what they call me, what matters is what I answer to.

I'll answer to John, to John Coutis, to Johnno. I won't answer to any smartarse remark about my physical disability, just as I won't answer to 'little Johnny' or 'Jonathon'. I'm a John or a Johnno, and nowadays I make people aware of that.

How are
You Goin'?

I WATCHED AN INTERVIEW recently with Jesse Martin, the teenage adventurer who sailed single-handedly around the world. He was asked what would have happened if he hadn't made it home, if he'd been lost at sea. And he replied that it wouldn't have been a tragedy; the tragedy would have been if he had lived until he was 80 years old and never attempted to do what he wanted to do. If he'd lived to 80 and not been satisfied with his life, that would have been a tragedy.

That's exactly how I feel about my life. I'm doing what I want to, I'm loving what I'm doing. That's no tragedy.

John at three and a half.

OPPOSITE The boys: John, almost five, three-year-old Luke and their big brother Adam, aged seven.

Luke and John in March 1973.

The Coutis family in 1981: Luke, Gary, Adam, Evelyn, Kristy and John, aged 12.

Johnno at the wheel.

At school in 1977.

The Coutis boys. *Left to right*: Adam, Luke and John, with their cousins Peter and Paul, *standing*, and Frank with his bear.

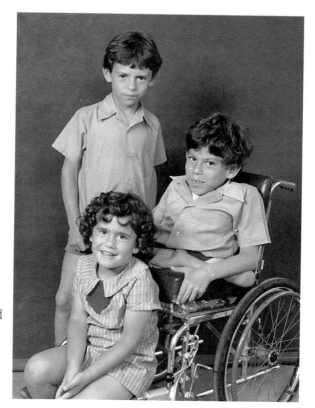

John, Kristy and Luke ready for school.

The gang – Luke, Kristy, Adam and John – in 1997.

John in his class photo of 1985.

Johnno on his trusty skateboard with his nieces Amanda, *left*, and Kimberley, 1999.

Best mate Matthew Anderson in 1995.

John with his Nan, Liberty Coutis, in 1999.

The sportsman
ABOVE The NSW Wheelchair Rugby League team in 1991.

OPPOSITE Coaching at a sports camp for the disabled, 1996.

BELOW In the National Table Tennis Championships in 1994.

Johnno and his great mate Stephen Waugh, 1994.

Great Britain's Olympic sprint champion Linford Christie and John coaching at a sports camp for the disabled in 1994.

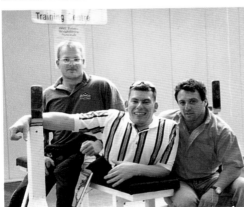

CENTRE With weightlifting coach Mr Bill 'Basil' Stellios, *right*, one of the biggest influences on John's sporting career, and Paul 'Hoover' Hyde, a 2000 Paralympian weightlifter and John's regular training partner between 1996 and 1999.

BELOW The Essendon AFL team in 1999. *Front row*: John with Bombers captain James Hird and coach Kevin Sheedy.

John's surrogate mother on many weekends, Bev Waugh, in 1996.

Mates from the Australian cricket team at the airport in 1994.
Left to right: Gavin Robertson, Jo Angel, Glenn McGrath and
Gavin's daughter Brittany.

Trish van Leeuwen, General Manager of WA Netball in 1996. This is one of John's favourite photos of his wife.

Greg Burke, *West Australian*, 5 June 1996

Trish and John at the dress rehearsal for the opening ceremony of the 2000 Sydney Olympics.

The wedding day, 1 July 2000.
Fern Fine Photography

John with his parents on his wedding day.
Fern Fine Photography

OPPOSITE The wedding cake, especially designed by Trish, featured the bride and her groom with no legs.
Fern Fine Photography

Groomsman Paul Dyett, Trish, John and his best man Stephen Waugh.
Fern Fine Photography

Speakers for the 1997 World Masters of Business and their guests.
Left to right: Rodney Adler, Brad Cooper, General Norman Schwarzkopf,
Brian Tracey, Ross Marlow, Lee Iacocca, Stephen Covey and Alan Jones,
with John in front.
World Masters of Business 1997

John and his
adopted uncle
Mr Alan Jones,
at radio station
2UE in 1998.

Great mates and colleagues Lisa Curry-Kenny, John and Grant
Kenny, 1997.
Winning Edge Seminars, Vision Ltd

After-presentation get together. Johnno and students from Penrhos
College, Perth, in 1999.

John with the Magan family. Mike Magan arranged for John to visit and speak to groups in Ireland in 2000. *Back*: Mike, Mary, Louise, Dan. *Middle*: Alice, Jonathan, Paula and James.

Trish and John on a double-decker bus driving through London, 2000.

Speaking at National Young Leaders' Day, Sydney Convention
Centre, 1999.
Highlife Education Ltd

John and Trish.
Janet Craig, Premier Studio, WA

Everyone is disabled in some way, physical or otherwise. Some might have asthma, some people might be epileptic, some might use hearing aids or have heart problems. What I often find, especially with rebellious teenagers, is that their so-called disability is their attitude, the lack of confidence or false bravado that prevents them from doing the things they dearly want to do. Not what they need to do, but what they want to do. If, when I'm giving a talk, I can change one person's attitude, get rid of one person's disability, then I've had a terrific day. I can't set out to change every attitude – though wouldn't that be great? – but one person, that should be possible.

One day not too long ago, at a shopping centre, I walked into an elevator that was packed with kids and adults from a variety of ethnic backgrounds. There were Italians and Asians, Lebanese and Africans, the odd Pom and now there was a Greek. As the doors closed I noticed that the atmosphere in the lift was pretty bleak; everyone had the same thought – please let me get to my floor and out of here as quickly as possible. People didn't speak, they shuffled in their own little circle, while a few of the kids were talking in a language other than Australian, which is something I deplore when I'm on Australian soil, especially in this case because they were obviously sniggering about me. I stared at them as their parents told them to be quiet. And it did go quiet. Very quiet.

And then I smiled, looked around the lift, and asked loudly, 'So how is everyone today?'

It wasn't just that I spoke, but the way I spoke. 'I'm all

right. How are you goin'?' came a reply and by the time we were all on our way, we'd had a quick laugh or two and hopefully were a little happier for the experience. The other thing I'd done by saying g'day in this way was to say to everyone in the lift, especially those kids, that just because I was physically disabled didn't mean I couldn't say hello, hold a conversation, be myself, be happy. A friend told me recently that because of the way I greet people they can tell that I'm a happy, positive person who is able to look after himself. When I was in that lift, by asking people how they were going and being positive I believe I was doing those people a favour, and I was doing myself a good turn too. I can't stress how important I find it to let people know that I am normal. Opinionated, often loud and always very short, but in essence the same as everybody else.

My 'able-bodied' schooling started in fifth class, but before that I was in a daycare centre for kids with disabilities – mental and physical. I was really lucky as far as the students of that centre went, because I was one of two, maybe three, who got to hop on a bus every afternoon and go home.

I was four or five years old when I first entered that daycare centre. I guess, strictly speaking, 'institution' is the correct term for the place, but because I was only there during the day I called it a daycare centre and for the purpose of this story I'll keep doing that. The centre was different things for different kids, depending on their disability and situation.

We learnt many things there – how to read and write, how to throw dusters into fans, how to play wheelchair sport. The first thing I discovered, however, was that there were other disabled children in this world. Remember, this was at a time when many thought it was better that disabled people weren't heard *or* seen. I had always been told that I was an able disabled person, like everyone else, different but able. Now I was relieved in a way to know that there were other disabled kids around. And shocked to discover just how brutal some kids' disabilities were. I was quickly impressed, and I think a little inspired, by the way many of these kids fought and overcame their disabilities. By the time I left, at the age of ten, to go to an 'able-bodied' primary school, I was very proud to have been part of that centre. And I was feeling a bit guilty, too, because I knew that many of my friends wanted to get out into the real world, but they couldn't.

Right from the start I was a bastard of a child at the centre. I quickly worked out that if you hide in cupboards and yell 'Boo!' when the cupboard door opens, you can scare the daylights out of people. I did so many wheelies on my wheelchair that they put weights on the wheels to slow me down. One terrible ruse I used for a while involved arriving every morning and complaining that I hadn't had breakfast yet. This was a straight lie, but I didn't care. I was offered a range of cereals and toast, a treat that lasted for a few days until one of the centre staff rang Mum and Dad to have a go at them. 'What are you talking about?' my Dad cursed back down the phone. I was given a lesson in the virtues of honesty when I got home that night.

I also had my first real crush on a girl at the centre. She was a library assistant, in her early twenties I guess, with a thick Canadian accent. I was devastated when she left; I thought she was stunning. But whether she really was a good sort I can't tell you – I thought that Alf from the TV show was a stunner in those days, too.

There was never one moment at that centre when I set out to show that I was less disabled than my comrades. If anything, I played on my disability because I came to learn that the staff were there to help and make things easier. It took years for that habit to be knocked out of me.

I had a good mate at that daycare centre, a bloke called Ken Paterson. Kenny was a young man with cerebral palsy, which is a disease that affects your body much more than your mind. You can have CP mildly or you can have it really badly – to the point that you cannot even move around under your own steam, can't communicate, can't do much at all. There is a vast range between mild sufferers and severe sufferers.

Kenny was right in the middle. He couldn't talk but he could communicate. When you were talking to him and you actually connected with him, you could see his eyes light up. Kenny had a keyboard in front of him, not really like a computer keyboard but a small keyboard with letters on it, and he had a stick in his mouth with a little ball on the end. With these he used to spell his words out to you. If he was telling you a joke or a story, it could take ages, and Kenny was really bad at telling long jokes. But when he finished, and you laughed out loud, his eyes would light up so brightly. He was one tough customer was Kenny Paterson, a lot tougher than you or me.

When I was dropped home after my day at the centre, I'd run up the driveway to be greeted by my mother. She would give me a hug, ask me how my day was, and point me towards the milk and cookies or cake she had ready for me. Kenny used to be on that same bus. But he never went home. Instead he went to another place where a lot of the kids with CP lived, those who needed to get appropriate care. Some of these kids wouldn't even go home on weekends; they'd go home once a month. A few never even got to go home. Yet here I was going home *every* afternoon. How lucky was I!

My parents were worried that if I remained at the daycare centre I wouldn't learn anything, wouldn't grow as a person. That I'd become a 'couch potato' who couldn't do anything with his life. So they fought with the school authorities, the bus companies, the local parents and citizens group – you name it, they fought 'em – until they finally had me enrolled in an able-bodied school. Dad had to take his handyman skills to the school to make a few minor adjustments, put a ramp in here and a ramp in there, and he made a couple of adjustments to the facilities in the toilet blocks, and then I was on my way.

Liberty Coutis: They didn't want to take kids like John. But Gary talked to them and got around them, so he went there. The public school wouldn't take him.

Gary Coutis: He wanted to learn, his mind was fine, his upper body was fine, and he wasn't handicapped. If he'd stayed there [at the daycare centre] it would've been no good. John needed to go to a school that was going to teach him something. The teachers at the special school were too busy with all the other kids that needed their help. John's other two brothers were already at the school. I had to tell them again and again, 'He doesn't need a special teacher.' I tried to tell them that mentally, John was fine.

For two years after I started at primary school, the bus company wouldn't let me on board to get to and from school. They were scared that I'd get hurt and they'd be involved in a lawsuit. I wasn't happy, and Dad was very unhappy, but my brothers were rapt because it meant we all got a lift to school with Dad every morning.

It was bloody hard making that transition from an institution to a school. I had been so pampered at the daycare centre; now I was the same as everyone else, only much more unprepared for that experience than all those around me. I was still getting a lot of attention, but much of it was unwarranted and some of it downright cruel. Initially I was the only physically disabled person at school, though when I moved to high school I was joined by a girl who got around with the aid of callipers on her legs.

In my school life I copped a barrage of name-calling and physical abuse, which turned me into a hard bastard. I had to be or I wouldn't have survived. But I don't mean hard as in some kind of brutal hitman. No, I had to learn to ignore people. Listen to them, laugh at them and walk away. Turn the other cheek. That's hard.

During the first week I was in primary school I got chased around the schoolyard by half-a-dozen bullies. When they caught me, they tied me up with a piece of rope, picked me up and threw me straight in the rubbish bin. Not one of those little bins you used to leave out the front for the garbageman, but one of those big metal rubbish bins that find themselves out the back of most schoolyards. When I landed among the wads of paper, garbage bags and rotting food, my first thought was, How the hell am I going to get out of here? But then things got much, much worse. The bastards set the bin on fire.

If it wasn't for the teacher who was doing playground duty, I would have been incinerated. There I was in that burning bin, hearing the crackles, smelling the smoke, the heat was getting extremely intense. I was all of 11 years old and I was about to die. But the teacher saw what was going on and rushed over, pulled me out, untied me and together we sat there and watched the bin burn itself out.

Going to high school brought a whole series of adjustments, and a new series of challenges. First, some simple maths. The primary school had 300 kids, the high school had 1700. That's a colossal 3400 high-school legs as against a mere 600 at primary school.

In high school the day was divided into eight periods of 40 minutes, with recess and lunch thrown in. I'll never forget one period with a casual art teacher. I reckon I'd only been a high-school student for around a month.

Now, if you're studying art, there are any number of things you could do in 40 minutes. You could paint, you could draw, you could work with clay. But what did this teacher do? She made us sit there and watch her riveting slide collection from a recent holiday in New Zealand! Whenever I hear a Kiwi sheep joke I chuckle and think back to that slide show because we saw a lot of bloody sheep that day. Halfway through the lesson I suddenly got a terrible pain in the stomach and needed to go to the toilet. I put my hand up, but she couldn't see me because she was concentrating too hard on her description of some hot spring in Rotorua. So, I thought, I'll just sneak out. After all, I didn't want to yell out, 'Scuze me, Miss, I've gotta go for a piss.' So I did what I thought was the right thing. I slid silently down off the chair and started making my way outside. But every single step I took, no matter how little or how big it was, was excruciatingly painful. I wasn't sure why, but self-preservation instincts told me that I was in no position to stop. I just had to grit my teeth and keep going.

I finally made it outside, shut the door and sat down on the floor. Then, slowly, I looked at my hands and could not believe what I saw. These bullies in my class had spread thumbtacks around my chair, so by the time I got outside I had three, four, five in one hand, four, five, six in the other.

Why hadn't I stopped and said, 'Ouch. What's going on?' And what, be humiliated in front of everybody? Be the laughing stock of the class, of the school? I don't think so. Yes, there was a little bit of pain, there was a little bit of blood, but you know what? There was also a lot of pride in me, in my heart. I didn't want *them* to get the best of me. I was at this school to stay, no matter what they did to me. I didn't want to give up. I took the tacks out, one by one, then struggled painfully up to sick bay, got a cab charge and went home.

I was confused, annoyed, depressed – so many different things. The pain in my hands was nothing compared to the hurt in my heart. I went into my bedroom and shut the door. I looked at myself in the mirror and bawled my eyes out. I didn't sob, I didn't cry, I bawled. I couldn't handle my situation any more, couldn't handle all the crap that was going on in my life, what people were saying, what people were doing. My brothers and my sister were hearing snide remarks, cruel jokes. My Mum and Dad were copping flak. Even my grandmother was being criticised by know-alls who believed my parents were doing things all wrong.

I looked at myself in the mirror again. I didn't want to go on. Right there, I thought about ways of killing myself.

How am I going to do it?

When will I do it?

Why?

Why not?

Who will I leave behind?

Does that matter?

And all the while, I was bawling, bawling, bawling.

Finally I decide. I was going to kill myself. That night. My life was about to be over. I bawled some more. I was scared, terrified, sad, confused, lonely, determined.

Then I heard a knock at the door, and my brother Luke walked in. He was ten years old, a couple of years younger than me. Luke could tell I'd had a shocker of a day. He didn't say anything, probably didn't know what to say. He sat down next to me, looked straight at me.

'Luke,' I whispered. 'I can't handle it any more. I'm going to kill myself. I'm going to end my life.'

My little brother didn't say a thing. Nothing. He just got up and started walking towards the door.

'Where are you going?' I said meekly. 'I've just told you I'm about to kill myself and you're walking away. Where are you going?'

He stopped at the door and looked back. 'I'm going to get the gun,' he said.

Luke was ten years old; he had no idea. Neither did I. I was 12.

A bit later my Mum came in. She sat down on the bed next to me and looked at me. She'd been crying; her eyes were soaked; she looked like I felt. Still she didn't say anything, just looked at me. Then she gave me one of those special huge hugs only mothers can give. You know the type of hugs I'm talking about. Mum pulled me close, gave me a kiss on the forehead and then, finally, she spoke. 'John,' she whispered, 'you are the most beautiful thing that has ever happened in our lives. Ever.'

Half an hour earlier I had been going to kill myself.

Now that seemed such a selfish, arrogant and disgusting thing to do. My Mum left and I cried some more. But these were different tears. I was still hurt, still angry, still unhappy. But I was loved.

I had much to live for.

An hour later my Dad arrived home. I was still in my room, though I was feeling a lot better. Dad came in and straightaway he roughed me up as he often did, one of those father–son rumbles where throughout the son feels as if he might be winning. Then, with one firm grip of Dad's hand on my shoulder, the rumbling stopped and Dad looked right into my eyes.

'Son,' he said sternly, 'no matter how big those guys are, you need to be taller and stronger than they are. You are going to have a lot of challenges in your life and you will be able to deal with every one of them. There'll be a lot of challenges.

'If I can do it,' he continued, 'why can't you?'

I love my Dad to death. I went back to school the next day, copped some more negative crap, but I wore it, always knowing that I had more style and more class and more courage than my antagonists.

When I look back over my life, there are long stretches – months at a time – that have slipped into the backstreets of my memory. Yet those couple of hours when I decided to end my life remain rock-solid in my consciousness. I remember my desperation, my despair, my emptiness, my fear. And I remember the comfort, the hope and the salvation my family offered.

It wasn't easy for my parents. One day, after my Dad had copped a few sledges from people who thought they knew more about how I should be raised than what he did, he grabbed me and asked flatly, 'Son, are you happy?'

Now, I was around 12 years old and going okay, doing things I never thought I'd be able to try, let alone achieve. 'Dad, I am,' I told him honestly. 'I'm having a great time. What are you worried about?'

'I just wanted to make sure,' he said.

'I love you, Dad,' I told him.

Legless

I MADE UP MY mind to get my legs amputated one month before my eighteenth birthday, on 14 July 1987. I decided to do so for one main reason – to help John Coutis.

I wanted to give myself more manoeuvrability, more mobility, more independence. It was one of the hardest decisions I have ever had to make, or will ever have to make. Yet there is no doubt in my mind that it was the best move I've ever made in my life.

I know many people have to make personal decisions that can be life-changing, or even life-threatening. What I faced was pretty serious stuff, too. Forget false modesty, I am very proud of myself because I made the decision and then went and *did* it. There are so many people who decide on a course of action, no matter how big or how small it might be, but don't follow through. That's one of my pet hates. I made my decision to have my legs amputated and then I went and did it.

I know I'm sounding repetitive, but, again, the way I was raised played a key part in this process. Mum and Dad taught us all to back our judgment and to move on and deal with situations. They helped us make decisions when we were young – we'd be backed even if our judgment was astray, so long as we hadn't been stupid, cruel or impetuous. If we were any of those things, they made sure we learnt from our mistakes. If it was up to us, then it was up to us.

Gary Coutis: We didn't hide John, we just took him straight out to the footy with us. I suppose one of the big things is we all went to the football together ... He used to get a lot of snickers, stares, names ... 'spastic' ... 'cripple' ... we just taught him to look the other way. I was pretty hard-nosed, you know, they dare not say anything to me because I don't know what I would have done.

We knew he was going to handle it before we got there. We educated him to turn the other cheek. We taught him to take it on the chin. We taught him that he was going to be called names, people were going to stare at him, poke fun at him ... he learnt to accept that when he was very young.

We just took him out and around and to beaches, camping, and threw him in the drink and taught him to swim. I taught John to walk on his hands. He'd take one step and then another step. He was like any kid being taught to walk, just happened to be on his hands. Then he started getting sores on his feet. That's when we had to start teaching him to walk on his hands and get his arse up and keep his feet from dragging on the ground, because he kept 'scabbing' them.

Until they were gone, my legs were a big part of my life, but for all the wrong reasons. I went through thick and thin with them. I had them dragging around behind me, my toes often getting infected from the way I had to drag them along the ground. The bullies at school saw me as an easy target.

Today I can stand in front of a mirror, see myself with no legs, and say, 'That's fine.' Inevitably not all the world sees me like that. The world is a weird, strange and wonderful place, and some people just can't handle the fact that there are many things that aren't quite as they seem.

I had a lot of good times at school, but some times were not so good. High school was tough. When I finished the first week, Dad said to me, 'Son, how was it?'

'Geez, Dad,' I replied, 'it was like a forest. It's scary, all those legs were like trees, moving around, waiting to squash me.'

I realised then that not only did I have to look after myself, I also had to look after other people. Too often, they had no idea I was down there, desperately dodging out of their way.

For a while, I took my wheelchair to school. The chair

had worked okay at the little primary school, and was a good idea in theory, but every time I struck a staircase at this big, bloody high school I found it quicker and easier to jettison the wheelchair and just scurry up the stairs. And I hadn't counted on the twisted minds of a mob that ruled the high-school quadrangle. I reckon that wheelchair was pulled apart at least 90 times, by angry teenagers who hunted as a pack and thought they were a lot tougher than they actually were. I'm not just talking about a few minor repairs – everything was taken apart, needing to be reassembled. In the end I could do the repair work with my eyes closed. Taught myself. Had to. Another time, they killed the brakes, which left me out of control after I inno-cently began wheeling down a ramp. It was lucky the maths teacher had left his window open, because I flew through it, straight into the staff room. What else did I cop? Being told my mother must have had sex with a frog was one particularly sick 'joke' that was repeated too often, but the one I remember most grievously was the incident that finally confirmed for me that I should get my legs amputated.

It was Year 9. The half-yearly geography exam. All up, there were 277-and-a-half young punks in that assembly hall – I don't know why I remember that number, but I do. We piled into that hall, the noise of sneakers and running shoes scuffling on the polished floorboards making it sound like some sort of gigantic basketball game.

Once everyone was positioned at their allotted table, the teacher said, 'Students, begin.' And we were away. I had climbed up onto my desk and was leaning on my elbows as I always did when I had to do any writing, still do today, with the exam paper in front of me, pen writing furiously and my brain working overtime. In what seemed like no time, the teacher said shrilly, 'Students, pens down.'

Before I take this story any further, I must explain the feelings I would get in my legs. Basically the limbs were useless. But if I could see you touching my legs, I could feel something. However, if I was concentrating on something else – reading a book, watching footy, doing an exam – I didn't feel a thing. Sadly, these bullies knew that. I had been sitting in that auditorium – as I said, propped up by the elbows, rest of my body jutting out, not sitting on the chair at all – thinking my absolute hardest. Now, as I slumped back onto the chair, I thought I'd done okay. I reckoned I was going to pass.

As soon as permission was granted, I jumped down and walked out on my hands into the sunshine. Almost immediately, a couple of the girls came up, a bit sheepishly, and said, 'John, can't you feel anything? Quick, look at your legs.'

What I saw was ghastly. I was amazed, I was shocked, I was distraught, I was angry, I was mad, I was sad and I was astounded at the state of my feet. They had been cut open by razor blades, been burnt by cigarette lighters, there were pins jabbed in them. A couple of toes had almost been severed. It was as if I was some kind of voodoo doll. It was awful, worse than acutely embarrassing, for I had not felt the pain until that moment, or seen the blood, bone, burn marks. These bastards had got at me in a most macabre and despicable way. I vowed then that I had to do something; I couldn't let my body be abused like that. I wasn't thinking revenge; it was more than that.

Having the legs amputated was a big call, a couple of years later, for a near-18 year old – lopping off what for most is half your body. But as I've said, it turned out to be the smartest thing I ever did.

From the hall, I made my way up to the sick bay, by this stage feeling more than a little queasy. The teachers wrapped a few bandages around the wounds before sending me off by ambulance to hospital, where I got patched up properly. Then I headed home, not to tell my parents how well or badly I'd gone in the exam but to tell them, finally, that the legs were going. First up, of course, my Old Man was ropeable. I thought he was going to go straight down to the school and find the pricks who'd attacked me. I have never, ever, seen my Dad so angry. However, I was past that stage and wanted to talk about my future. 'I've been thinking about this for a long time now,' I told them calmly. They knew then that I was going to talk to them about my legs, for they had been the subject of some discussions in the past. 'But after today, I've got to do it.'

We talked about it some more and came to the conclusion that, while it was best to wait until I'd finished school, it was – if that's what I really felt was best – the right thing to do. This process reflected one of the best characteristics of my parents. They would always offer advice to their children and argue their opinions if they conflicted with ours, but as we kids grew older and the decisions got tougher, we actually got to make those decisions for ourselves. And we lived with the consequences.

You know, whenever I think about that incident in that geography exam, one thing that amazes me is that as far as I know no one was ever punished for the crime. I can't imagine what marks those bastards got for that exam. Clearly they'd been more concerned with attacking me whenever the teachers were looking the other way than getting as many marks as they could. For accomplices they had all the spineless students who'd been sitting near me; no way could they not have noticed what was going on. I don't know who did it, but what is strange is that I'm not sure the school ever went out of their way to find out who was responsible. Maybe they figured it was my fault or perhaps they were frightened to discover how sick some of the minds in that Year 9 might have been. For me, though, it's in the past; I can't change it. It's for other people's consciences to worry about. I've moved on.

I have other unfortunate memories from school, such as one teacherless day when four guys grabbed me, tied me to the ceiling fan in one of the classrooms, and switched it on. I felt like Kermit the bloody frog, absolutely helpless. And then, after they finally turned the fan off, they left me there. How did I get off? Too proud and embarrassed to cry for help, I just fell onto the floorboards and bounced a few times. Don't know how I didn't hurt myself. I guess I was lucky.

There are others, but that's enough. Of course many of

these experiences were truly awful, but they did teach me perseverance, how to handle things. I needed this to get to where I am today. Such cruelty toughened me up, but it also taught me to properly value those who truly cared. And as much as anything, the weight of those schoolyard incidents, and especially that Year 9 geography exam, made me realise I'd be better off without those legs.

Everyone who's struggled but climbed out of his or her misfortune has a turning point, and for me that moment came when I began to stop thinking so poorly of myself. Helped by others, especially my parents, I told myself that I needed to stop blaming other people. The decision to have my legs amputated signified this. I needed to stand up for myself, but also be cool and not try to change what couldn't be changed. Part of that was being able to laugh. Also, my Dad taught me that I shouldn't bottle up my emotions or waste them by expressing them inappropriately – and it probably saved my life.

The decision to have my legs amputated was mine and mine alone. I discussed it with three people – Mum, Dad and my doctor. Everyone else, I either told them I was going to do it or waited until after it was done and let my new physical appearance talk for itself. My brothers and sister backed my judgment, as did my closest friends. To a person, their view was that if I knew it was the right thing to do then go for it. Mum and Dad were the same, though they took time to make sure I was thinking clearly. The doctor did no more than explain the risks and the pros.

Dr Warwick Mackay: After John came to me and told me he wanted to get rid of his legs, I said to him, 'Yep, you're legs *are* useless, let's get rid of 'em.' I referred him to [the late] Dr Barry Collins and he amputated both those sad little stumpy legs on 14 July 1987.

I thought John getting his legs amputated was a very sensible move. I could see they were useless to him. I knew it was going to be a big decision for him. And we always get worried when anyone has an elective amputation, because occasionally – it rarely happens but when it does it can be a horrendous complication – the patient can suffer phantom limb pain afterwards. The last thing we wanted was for John to live a life with phantom limb pain. He did have some phantom pain the first 12 months, but now it only happens very rarely, maybe once a year. Having a positive attitude helps.

He had come to the conclusion that he could walk around on his hands. They became his legs. His brain was wonderful. He knew how to get on in life . . .

For an able-bodied person, it would take a long time to come to terms with having a leg or legs amputated. You have a prosthesis put on, either above or below the knee. You've got to learn to walk again. But this bloke was already walking on his 'legs', only they were his arms. John got rid of his useless appendages that were in his way. He was getting pressure ulcers on them all the time, skin infections and he would have got osteomyelitis [an inflammation of the bone and bone marrow, caused by infection], which could have caused life-threatening complications.

When he 'walked', after the operation, he had greater ground clearance, and because of the way his legs used to splay out before tucking in underneath his torso, he wasn't as 'wide' anymore either.

Let's do it.

After the operation to remove my legs, while I was still groggy from the anaesthetic, I clearly remember moving my hands, very slowly, down to where my legs once had been. There was nothing under the sheets. I lay there for hours, many hours, thinking, Wow, I've really done it, I've got them out of the way. What a momentous step forward! You know those dreams you have when you wake up and you think, That was real, or Did that actually happen? This was like that – only it really *had* happened.

The physical aspect of the recovery process was a battle in itself. I had to work out, all over again, how to find and then retain my balance. I had to learn to 'walk' again. Everything you take for granted, that I had taken for granted, I had to learn again. How to get into chairs, climb onto beds, up and down stairs, go to the toilet – I had to learn it all. Never underestimate your ability to balance. I had to teach myself again how to eat at a table without having half my meal ending up on the carpet. By the time I left hospital, three-and-a-half weeks after the surgery, I could do most of these things. I couldn't wait to get out of that ward so I could tackle the world and start living again.

When I came out of hospital I still had staples in my legs but within three days I was playing indoor cricket, which was a real passion of mine, had been for years (but more of that later). I even bled on the court a bit, but I was just so keen to get on with living. You can only imagine the reaction of the guys at the indoor cricket centre. One day I was there, complete with legs, albeit dud ones. Then I was gone. And then I was back, without legs. 'Shit, what happened to you!' they gasped as one.

I told them straight and they replied, 'What a bloody hard decision.' Nothing I could say could convince them that it really wasn't that hard. But they hadn't been living with those legs. At the time it was the best decision of my life (making up my mind to get married has moved into the top spot now), but nothing I could say could convince these able-bodied people of that simple fact.

Trish van Leeuwen (John's wife): To this day, whenever John and I go to Richmond to visit John's Nan, we always drive past the hospital where he had that operation. 'Look, Trish,' he'll say, 'there's my room, and there's where they lopped my legs off.' It's an important signpost in his life.

It's a fact of life that everyone of us is able to be hurt in some way, shape or form, whether it be by something said, something done, or something physically inflicted. The truth is that this world is full of hurt. Everywhere you look people are being punished; someone is upset or crying. As

I learnt so clearly during this period of my life, people should be hugging, not struggling with pain.

I guess I could have taken the easy way out and stayed indoors, saying, 'God, look what they've done to me. I can't go on. I'm not going out of this safe house any more, I'm just going to lock myself away.' In a way, I think I was entitled to turn my back on the world. That was not how I was raised, but it would certainly have been the easy option. I knew that. I thought about doing it, I've got to tell you; it crossed my mind on more than one occasion. On numerous occasions. But I said to myself, sometimes shouted to myself, 'No, bugger it. You're not gonna beat me.' And they didn't. I beat them.

Joe Hutton: One of the aspects about John that I love – and sometimes it gets a less than positive reaction from others – is when sometimes people have said to him, 'No you can't do that.' Whether that has to do with his disability or that's the rules, you're just not allowed to do that., I've seen John go, 'Nup, we're going to do that. Stuff you. Let's just do it.'

The day I finished school was a big day for me. That part of my life was finished; a new adventure was about to begin. I'd overcome some bloody big hurdles to reach that point, been through some horrendous experiences, enjoyed some wonderful moments, and now it was time to meet some fresh challenges. The real world awaited.

Evelyn Coutis: He's worked for the whole time since he left school. We made him go to work and earn money, made him pay for his first car with his own money.

I had a little bit of packing experience from when we used to do the shelves in Dad's take-away shop, so I went out looking for this kind of work. I must have knocked on a million doors, until finally the owner of a local hardware store, one of the good guys of the neighbourhood, said, 'Yeah, orright. We'll give you a go.' I'm glad he did, but I wish he hadn't, too, if you know what I mean. By the end of the day I was absolutely rooted. I don't think my new boss had given any thought to what I could and couldn't do, and neither had I. Maybe I'd talked up my abilities a bit too much. When I was told to 'do this' I tried to do it, no matter how impossible it was for me to do, and by long before stumps on that first day I knew this wasn't for me. To amuse myself, I remember putting myself up on the shelves a couple of times, but no one wanted to buy me. Less funny was the moment when I was required to put full paint tins that were taller and heavier than I was on the shelves. At day's end, I took my eight hours worth of pay and went on my way, wiser for the experience. I still wanted to conquer the world, but I had to be realistic – this was one of the first times I really noticed that I couldn't do everything that everybody else could do. In this regard, things were going to be a little bit tougher in my adult life than they had been in the schoolyard.

Fortunately, I was able to quickly find another job, at a

place called Butler & Reardon. Everyone in the electricity game has heard of Butler & Reardon. It is the company that makes all the meter boxes that are on the side of houses, units, factories, whatever. My job there was to put little bits and pieces together, for the combined parts to then be fitted inside the meter boxes. This was more to my capabilities.

I got that position thanks to my Uncle Con, who taught at a school in Blacktown, St Pat's College. The principal at St Pat's at the time was a champion called Brother Bernard, who'd taught one of the owners of Butler & Reardon. My uncle told me years later that Brother Bernard was owed a favour by the company and used it to get me a start. But there were no favours once I began. I had a job to do, and I was expected to do it. Both gigs – the day at the hardware store and the job at Butler & Reardon – were eye-opening experiences for me, strong lessons that I was not going to get it all my own way as I tried to make it in this world.

Not that I expected a bed of roses, but maybe I'd anticipated that working life was going to be a little bit easier than what it was. At Butler & Reardon I used to sit on a little stool and screw nuts and tie bolts, one after the other after the other – repetitive work that was only done because the boss said so and because the people doing the work had rents and grocery bills to be paid. After weeks of this I was promoted to a bigger machine, which offered more variety amid the monotony of it all. Still, Mum and Dad had always taught me to be as good at whatever I was doing as I could, so I tried my darnedest to get each and every job right. That philosophy rubbed off on all of us in the Coutis household, I reckon, and we all tried to apply it to our careers, our sport and our personal lives. The only tasks that beat me were the ones that, because of my physical limitations, I simply couldn't do.

I stayed at my Nan's during the week. I'd get up early, 4.30 am, catch a train into Blacktown, get off the train (which could be an adventure in itself), and then ride my skateboard from the station to work, a few kilometres away. After we knocked off for the day, I would either come home with my uncle or catch the train home and then head straight off to be paid to umpire indoor cricket matches at the local sports centre.

Liberty Coutis: Rather than Gary getting up at about four in the morning to bring John, who was working in Blacktown, down from North Richmond, John sometimes stayed with me. So I used to take him outside on the footpath and I watched him till he got down to the station and crossed the road. It was dark in winter and I was scared he was going to get knocked over because who would see him? So once he got to the station, because you could see it from the house, and he'd crossed the road, then I went inside. I was outside in my dressing gown waiting for him to cross the road. Spoilt little bugger he was.

Butler & Reardon wasn't a bad place. I learnt a bit about life and made a couple of good mates. I also started a university course that year, at the University of Western

Sydney, studying at night, which meant that I had plenty going on. If I wasn't working or studying, or playing or umpiring at the indoor cricket centre, I was having an early breakfast or sleeping.

My results at uni were pretty good, if I do say so myself. After four years, I ended up with a business diploma, majoring in commerce and marketing. Again, it was something that I wanted to do, to demonstrate that disabled people can do it, and hopefully to give me a chance to do something in business down the track. My Mum and Dad always stressed that I didn't have a mental disability. To be honest, I was never the greatest student; in fact, I hated reading then and I still do. I know this isn't the best thing for an author to reveal, but it's the truth. A lot of people pick up a newspaper and turn straight to the back page for the sport, or they rush to the gossip pages in the middle, or turn studiously to the finance and business section. Me? I go straight to the comics and then to the sport, from the sport I go to the gossip, from the gossip, I go to the news and business.

I did learn at school and especially at uni that if you put in the work, you do get results. I actually knuckled down late in my school life and picked up some quite respectable marks. This was pretty encouraging, another lesson about the value of perseverance. If you want it bad enough, stick at it. Much of it really wasn't *that* hard, though study had its moments, and there were times when I just wanted to throw it all in. But whenever I thought this, I told myself, no, it'll be worth it in the long run. And, it turned out I was right.

My time studying, at school and at uni, taught me a lot about myself – how smart (in an academic sense) I could be so long as I worked at it – and how resourceful the human brain actually is. I learnt the value of planning, of looking ahead. I also saw countless examples of people assuming that because I had a physical disability I was mentally retarded as well. It was always nice to set them straight.

Meanwhile, to earn a living, I stayed at Butler & Reardon for around six months, until Dad set up a joinery business and gave me a job working in the office. Occasionally I'd go outside and help the lads in the factory a little bit but in the main I was taking phone calls, placing orders, doing the wages, dealing with the public, sales reps and others. That interacting with the public was important for me because it gave me confidence and also the chance to observe people and discover the best ways to deal with individuals.

For the next few years, that was how I paid my way, working at Dad's factory and then making a few bucks more umpiring indoor cricket at nights and on weekends. With study, sport and all the usual socialising that young blokes do, I had a busy life.

For a period in the early 1990s, I became closely connected with the Bankstown–Canterbury Cricket Club. My role was like that of a manager for the first-grade side, and I fielded every now and then when they were short. I always had my whites with me. So many kids would love to play first-grade cricket. How many kids with disabilities would love to? Every one of them. How many can say they have? Not too many, I reckon. I did everything I could for Bankstown and cherished the moment every time I ever walked out onto the field for them. In doing so, I was going from being a disabled person to being just like everybody else. That was important.

It's amazing. Almost everyone is told when they're young that if they work hard and apply themselves, they'll get somewhere, they'll achieve things. I know my Dad was forever telling me that during the late 1980s and well into the '90s, and I was forever replying, 'Yes, Dad. Of course, Dad.' But to be honest I never really applied myself until I was about 27 years old. Sure, there were times when I worked hard, at uni, in sport, at work, but I didn't really dedicate myself to anything I did except, perhaps, my sport, until then. In my immature eyes, life was too rosy for working *that* hard; I was having a good time. Dad would say, 'If you want it that bad, try that little bit harder, try that *little* bit harder.'

As I got older, as I discovered what 'it' was, I did try that little bit harder and things started happening for me. Things started falling out of the sky for me. That wasn't luck. That was Dad's advice coming true.

Today I never use a wheelchair; I get around on my own or on my faithful skateboard. One funny thing about this skateboard is that kids love it. I've had lots of offers for it; in fact, I could have sold it so many times I'd be set up for life now. Occasionally, I find myself in discussions with other skateboard fiends, talking as if we're debating the merits of different models of hot rods.

I haven't seen too many people who get around on a skateboard as I do. The idea of using one evolved from my time at the daycare centre, when I often rode about on what we called a 'prome board'. This was a low-to-the-ground board that was more to my shape, wide at the bum end of it, with wheels that weren't too dissimilar to the wheels that propel shopping trolleys. This meant, of course (we all know what bloody shopping trolleys are like), that the prome board could go in all directions, often against my will. But despite sometimes careering off east when I wanted to go west, I quickly worked out how to take care of myself and to get around on the lino floors pretty rapidly.

In those days, when I wasn't at the centre, I used a wheelchair. And when I left to go to primary school I left the prome board behind, so other kids could use it. Meanwhile, someone – I honestly can't remember who; it might have been Dad, might have been the woodwork students at school – made me a similar sort of board, only wider and with wheels from roller skates.

This board was terrific in many ways. For one thing, it only went backwards and forwards, so it didn't have a mind of its own like the prome board – but I didn't have it padded like I do my skateboard today, so it could be cruel on my butt and murder on rough roads. Because there was plenty of rugged terrain at school I usually stuck to the wheelchair, but at home that board was excellent and became one of my closest friends. Then one day it dawned on me that a skateboard would do an even better job, so after talking to my Dad and brothers about what I needed to look for, I went out to buy one like a teenager going to Auto Alley to select his first car.

Since then I've had a few different skateboards. Just like cars, they've got better as technology has improved, to the point that now I go to my preferred skateboard specialist store and get one custom-made, with wheels the way I need them and the board upholstered the way I prefer. I have to change the bearings around every six months, which can be quite expensive. Fair dinkum, it costs me more to get my skateboard serviced than it does to get my car done!

With the skateboard, I get around okay. Trish, my wife, who has worked with disabled people for years, tells me that it might not be as easy for me in a lot of other countries, that from her experience Australia is a long way ahead of other nations when it comes to supporting the disabled. My experiences, though not as broad as hers, suggest the same.

Joe Hutton: One time that was pretty funny occurred at Brisbane Airport. We were waiting to get on the plane and John wanted to get on first. They called out, 'Anyone who needs a hand boarding or has a disability, please come up now, and the stewardess will assist you onto the plane.'

So we go up there, and John is on his skateboard. And on his skateboard he is very good; he can move through people, cars, up and down escalators and doesn't mind going fast. There was a long sloping walkway onto the plane and John did a big right-hand turn and flew straight down that walkway.

Halfway down, standing there, is the pilot talking on his mobile phone with his back to John coming down. John is going for this guy, and I'm going, 'He has to hear it; he's going to have to hear this skateboard coming.'

But he didn't. Just as John was about to bowl the captain out for a strike, the stewardess and I shouted, '*Watch out!*' The pilot turned around, and the look of fear on his face.

He did a 'star jump', and John skated straight underneath his legs. It was hilarious. The poor pilot just didn't know what had happened.

Whatever the circumstances, life as a physically disabled person is never going to be too easy. Take one example – automatic teller machines. Now here's a challenge. The first parking ticket I ever got came about because of an ATM. One weekend, with my new plastic card proudly in my pocket, I parked my car near the bank and raced up to the machine. Unfortunately I wasn't sure what to do, and even more unfortunately there was nowhere to jump up onto so I could read the instructions. I was on my own. What to do? It seemed my only alternatives were to remain broke until the bank reopened on the Monday, to Spider-man-like abseil up the wall, to sulk or to improvise.

Eventually I worked out what to do. I dashed back to my car and drove it up onto the footpath, with the front bonnet – no, that's not quite tall enough, better make it the roof! – slapbang in front of the ATM. Beautiful. Then I hopped out of my seat, jumped up through the sunroof, whacked my card into the hole in the wall, punched in my pin and was on my way. But while I was completing my transaction, a parking officer, 'Pat the Bomber' I called her, came along and booked me. She obviously thought I was just being an idiot. I understand she was only doing her job, and there was no doubt the car was illegally parked, but I've always wondered whether she might have been a little more understanding if she'd realised what I was about.

This Sporting Life

WHEN I WAS A KID, I wanted to play all the games that my brothers were playing. As I grew older, rather than thinking about those things that were impossible and really weren't that important, I focused on the sports I could play and tried my darnedest to be good at them. There's not much point wanting to play Rugby League for Australia if you're better suited to cricket or soccer. I realised that whether it was able-bodied sport or disabled sport, at the elite level it is all about competition, with the same adrenalin rushes, thrills and disappointments.

Gary Coutis: John wanted to play Rugby League like Adam, but I just told him what was going to happen. I said, 'Grow up, fella. You want to get out there? Look at the size of that kid; do you want him to come and fall on you?'

He looked at me and said, 'Wouldn't be real good, Dad.'

We told him it wasn't going to happen. We just said this is possible, but this...maybe not.

Before heading off to primary school, I was extremely lucky to be given the chance to be involved in a number of sports at the daycare centre. Until then sport had usually been something to watch from afar, because I just wasn't physically equipped to take part. If that daycare centre hadn't been switched on to sport – and I'm told that many aren't – who knows what I would have done with my competitive urges. Maybe they would have simply withered away. The centre was where I first discovered sports that I was good at, where I could have fun *and* be competitive. And, boy-o-boy, was I determined to win.

As I've explained, in my early years I used a wheelchair most of the time but eventually I progressed on to my skateboard. The wheelchair was good, a tough old thing that was built like a tank, and I used it like a tank every now and then, especially when I was playing wheelchair sports such as wheelchair Rugby League. It weighed around 30 to 35kg, with big, bulky wheels on the front. I used to paint it red, mainly for effect on the court, and place stickers all over it. It had no footplates because I took them off – they were no use to me. My old Sherman tank; it used to go all right.

From the day I was first introduced to wheelchair sports, that old chair of mine became one of my closest friends. I'd always loved sport so here was a way to live my own sporting life, and I quickly found that wheelchair Rugby League, in particular, was great. It's played on an open basketball or tennis court, with six per side – three in electric chairs and three in manual chairs. Thus, it is open for players with any disability – the electric guys with cerebral palsy or muscular dystrophy or brittle-bone disease or whatever they have; it's a game for everyone. It's a numbers game. We used a tennis ball (but any small ball would have done the job) in scrums and to kick goals. Players usually wear numbers and names on their jumpers. The ball is passed from player to player by calling out the number on their jumper or their name. With that wheelchair as my weapon, I used to think of myself as the Wally Lewis or Peter Sterling of wheelchair Rugby League. I had a bit of mongrel in me. I used to smash 'em, and even earnt the nickname of 'The Hammer' because I had no legs hanging over the front of the chair so I could charge straight in, metal first. I was so competitive.

Evelyn Coutis: He was pretty aggressive. He was really rude to the other players. Knocked 'em over and didn't care if he knocked them out of their wheelchairs. 'Serves 'emselves right,' he'd say.

We had some great dingles. I remember one opponent getting away down the sideline but I came across in cover,

81

leant down and grabbed his back wheel. We had this huge stack, both of us ending up in the grandstand. People in the crowd were chewing wheelchair parts for a month. I was okay, in this and any other crash, because if I got knocked out of my chair I just got back up and jumped back in. Some of these other guys, bloody wimps, I'd smash into 'em, they'd fall out of their chairs and couldn't get back up. What could I do, other than run over them as if they were a speed hump? Often there were complaints that I played it too hard, but I saw this as a simple reflection of their lack of commitment.

I prefer wheelchair Rugby League to wheelchair basketball. I played wheelchair basketball, but it wasn't as much a contact sport as its Rugby League cousin. Wheelchair League was often like dodgem cars the way I played it, like smash-up derbies. I guess my bias against basketball had something to do with my lack of height. Even when we were sitting in our chairs, I was a lot shorter than everybody else. I could still play, no problem at all, shoot goals and everything else, but I didn't enjoy it as much as wheelchair League. But a sport's a sport, so I gave it a go and had a good time doing so.

My best friend at this time was a bloke called Matthew Anderson. I originally met Matthew at the daycare centre. He was a couple of years younger than me, but with our mutual love of sport in general and our wheelchair Rugby League in particular, we just clicked. I actually played against him to start with, but our attitude to sport was the same, and we recognised that kinship very quickly. After a game we'd get together and talk about how it'd gone, about life, people with disabilities, Australia, everything. Like I said, we just clicked.

In the early 1990s Matthew and I both made a NSW side that played Queensland in wheelchair Rugby League. And didn't we smash those 'banana benders'! Matthew played in an electric wheelchair, and we worked really well together. He was a genius for reading the play; he knew what the other teams were going to do three or four tackles before they did it. When we had the ball, he knew how they'd defend and what we should be doing to keep the advantage. During one game we put on a shifty move, this way and that way, and then Matthew put one of our mates, Purcey, straight through a gap. He was off! There was no one in his sights, absolutely no one, and he should have scored for sure. But can you believe it!

Purcey's shoelace was undone and not far from the line it got caught in his front wheel. One more spin of the wheel and he was pulled out of the chair, straight over the top, and landed headfirst on the concrete. Then, adding pain and insult to pain and insult, his chair ran him over, nearly killing him. That was the only game we lost for a number of years, all because of that bloody shoelace.

It's a bit ironic, really, me being beaten by a shoelace!

That's one of my favourite sporting stories, but I'm getting ahead of myself. By the time I'd left primary school, I knew so many different things about myself – what games I could win, which ones I couldn't win, and which games I didn't really have to worry about competing in. For example, Luke and I always easily won the wheelbarrow race, absolutely carved 'em up. Then it was straight over to the piggyback race, which we'd always win as well. Mind you, we weren't lay-down misères because occasionally Luke would start running a bit too quickly, trip over and then it was carnage. You should never be too confident. All good fun.

At primary school I was more often than not reduced to being a spectator, except at the annual swimming carnival, when I was allowed to use my boogie board. This, I thought, was pretty cool. I'd dive off the blocks straight onto the board and away I'd go, unstoppable for the first part of the race. But if I fell behind, I couldn't cope with the other guys' backwash.

I did try other sports at high school, with different degrees of success. I was in a wheelchair for most of these. Archery was okay, so long as somebody went down and got the arrows for me. Shot put – most of the time *I* was the shot, rather than the person putting it. High jump – my best chance was for a teacher to throw me over the bar. Disciplines such as discus were just a bit too hard from the chair. Cross-country running and the uneven bars were right out. But I did play a lot of table tennis in high school, always against able-bodied classmates, which I saw as a challenge. I wanted to be as good as they were, and cringed whenever I was offered a start. I was very proud when I was nominated as captain for a couple of inter-school visits to play a Wollongong side, prouder still the time we won.

The sport that *really* grabbed my attention, even more than wheelchair Rugby League, was indoor cricket. I started playing indoor cricket when I was around 12. I turned up unannounced at the centre at nearby Windsor one day, armed with one of Uncle Con's old Slazenger bats, which Dad and I had sawn in half, and said I wanted to give it a go. My efforts were very much at the knockabout level until I had my legs amputated, but right from the start, I was a standout purely because I was so competitive, and I needed only some minor rule changes, despite the fact I was physically disabled. The rule alterations were simple – I'm half a person so I got to bowl from halfway down the wicket and when I batted I only had to run half as far to complete a single. I played with half a bat as well. And the no-ball rule (which covers whether a delivery is legal or illegal) was amended so that anything that was over stump high when it passed the batsman (me) was called no-ball by the umpire; otherwise bowlers would have been getting the ball to bounce that high every ball, thus keeping me scoreless. Some mugs who couldn't play the game treated these rules as a joke, but for the blokes with some ability these rule changes were a challenge. They had to concentrate hard and work out a different means of attack. For me, it was terribly challenging, and I loved it. I really enjoy playing disabled sports but, like the table tennis matches I played against anybody, this was better. From the time I realised that I could match it with able-bodied indoor cricketers, I've never classed myself as a disabled person, at least when it came to sport.

I'm as competitive as any cricketer I know. I recall infuriating a couple of blokes into trying to bowl at 160km an hour. And another fella started off bowling underarm lobs to me but by his second or third ball he was storming in at me. I was carting him all over the court; it was magic. My brother Luke was playing that night, and I can remember him politely pointing out to this bloke what a complete bloody goose he was. Hopefully, after he cooled down, the bloke had learnt a lesson about treating people as you find them, rather than how you originally perceive them.

One day at indoor cricket, I was asked if I wanted to play in one of the Windsor Indoor Centre teams which played League matches against representative teams from other centres. Of course I did, but would our opposition be okay with that? After all, they had never played under, let alone approved, the rules as I played them at Windsor. So the guys at Windsor approached the other teams, and no one had a problem, so I was in. I started at the bottom, in the lowest grade, but worked my way up and won a couple of titles in the process. Eventually I was promoted right up to the top grade, and from there went on to represent NSW, which was excellent.

At this highest level, though, I sensed that perhaps I wasn't as welcome as I'd been before. This is not a sledge against the cricketers as blokes – the treatment I received was tremendous. But I'm not sure if they knew exactly how to accept me as a cricketer on the court, and I think there was a bit of negativity towards the rule modifications that were in place to put me on an equal footing.

Perhaps they had a point. I had to keep remembering that I was playing their sport, they weren't playing mine.

And I wasn't making adjustments to my game for them while they were making plenty for me. But it was still good fun, and hard at times, too.

When it came to sledging, I mixed it with the best of them. But I came unstuck one night at Peakhurst, when I was into a bloke, kept at him and at him with some of my very best lines. He was a highly regarded player in outdoor grade cricket, but to me he was a bit too flash. And I hated the way he just ignored me.

When we came off after we'd fielded for our 16 overs, one of my teammates whispered to me, 'Shit, Johnno. What were you giving that bloke a mouthful for? Don't you know he's deaf?'

It must have looked real pretty, me getting into a bloke with a physical disability!

Eventually, my rep career came to an end, partly because the cricketers tired of the special rules under which I played, and partly because my body simply gave up on me. I was asking too much of it, playing too many games. I also had a sense that some people were suggesting that I was being picked *because* of my disability rather than because of my contribution to the team, a sort of reverse discrimination. I don't think that was true but I couldn't prevent others pushing that barrow.

Steve Waugh (best friend and the current Australian cricket captain): I never played indoor cricket against him, but I watched him play a couple of times. He was a tough captain. I saw him nail his own players if they didn't put in the way he wanted. He's a really good indoor cricketer, very competitive with a good cricket knowledge.

If John had been able-bodied, there's no doubt that he would have been at least a capable cricketer. With his catching, he's as good as anyone now. He's been to quite a few of our practice sessions – the Australian side and the NSW side – and he's caught everything that's been belted at him, no problem at all, no matter that ball has come off the bat at full pace. He's obviously a naturally talented sportsperson, with a fierce desire to win and play well.

I also had a couple of games of outdoor cricket in my late teens, with my cousin Frank's team, at good old Richmond Oval. Before that, I would go up there on Saturdays to score for the juniors. I think that's how Sir Donald Bradman started, too!

Although I'd put my table tennis racquet in the cupboard, when I was around 20, I got a call from a bloke who was involved in table tennis for the disabled and I was soon eager again for the ping-pong fray.

As far as table tennis was concerned, away from school I concentrated on the competition for the disabled at the elite level. Competition was tough, but it could be funny, too, such as the time, during a NSW championship, when I played against a 'vertically challenged' competitor. I was in a wheelchair; my rival wasn't – which meant that as I looked over the net all I could see were these two beady little eyes and half a paddle. It was as if I was up against Dicky Knee!

As usual I became a bit of a mongrel once the game began – all I wanted was to beat this guy. I played the corners a fair bit and used the drop shot judiciously, so that my little opponent was running all over the place. But no one had told me that competitors such as my opponent, who stood below a certain height but were still mobile on their feet, had a special rule that allowed them to get two bounces, not just one. I thought I was winning all these points with my clever drop shots but when I looked up at the scoreboard I was getting slaughtered. I had to change my game plan and work bloody hard to get those points back. We had a good laugh about that later.

I was the Australian disabled table tennis champion for three years from 1992 – playing from a table perched at the end of the playing surface rather than a wheelchair. Unfortunately, though, that was not quite enough to get me selected for the Atlanta Paralympics in 1996. The competition there involved only the top 12 in the world, plus a few wildcards, and though I worked my ranking down from No. 61 at the start of the year to No. 13, I missed out.

Then Matthew Anderson, my very best mate, died in tragic and, for me, devastating circumstances, which put the disappointment of not going to Atlanta completely in perspective.

After Matthew died, I took a break from the world for a while. I grew a beard, kept myself ordinary and out of the sun, and became something of a Bilbo Baggins, the reclusive character from my favourite book, Tolkien's *The Hobbit*. My competitive urges went away; I didn't care if I lost.

To a large degree, it was sport that finally brought me back into the world. I had met a few people who were involved in powerlifting, and I'd given it a go without ever getting serious at it. But in late 1996 it offered me the chance to stay fit and take out a few frustrations. After I got over my disappointment at missing out on Atlanta I looked at the weights and thought that they might be a way to participate in the Paralympics in Sydney, 2000. So I got fair dinkum about the sport and discovered that I absolutely loved it. I was offered a scholarship through the Australian Institute of Sport, which I accepted, and then I began moving through the grades.

When I started powerlifting seriously, I was a fat porker, weighing around 45kg, which is plenty for me. Before my first competition, I looked at my rivals, paid attention to what weights they were lifting, and thought, This shouldn't be too difficult. But how wrong I was. There's a lot more to this sport than meets the eye, in terms of technique, strategy and mental strength. I found that I could barely lift my own body weight, which wasn't even close to being competitive.

However, after a few months' hard training, working with a terrific coach Bill Stellios and a lifting partner in Paul Hyde, who really brought the best out of me, I was on my way. Paul has represented Australia and was a whiz for teaching me so much about concentration, mental toughness, perseverance, and dealing with injuries. With his help I ended up lifting a personal best in competition of 125kg. I'm sure that if fate hadn't ended my run, I would now be lifting a whole lot more.

Dr Warwick Mackay: When he really started to get into the weightlifting, he used to tell me he was going to the gym. And I'd be into him. 'You're going to hurt your legs [his arms]!' And eventually he did. He hurt his arms by straining too hard on those weights. He even broke his 'knee' – his elbow – by going too hard.

He's got obsessive traits in his personality, which is the only way he's survived. A lot of people with his gross abnormalities wouldn't have made it; they wouldn't have gone past five or six years of age. He had it in his brain to live and to survive.

I loved the camaraderie that built up between us. Whenever I walked into the gymnasium at the New South Wales State Sports Centre, it was as if I was part of a special family, which in a sense was exactly what we were – a family of elite athletes. We knew when to muck around and have fun but we knew, too, how to spur each other on to greater efforts. I kept at it until 1999, when I was struck by a serious illness and my dreams for 2000 were ruined. I'll write more about that damn illness a little later. Maybe one day I'll get back into it, but even if I don't I'll always have those memories of mixing with so many great athletes and proving to myself that I was up there among them.

Lisa Curry-Kenny (former Olympic swimmer, now successful businesswoman and inspiring public speaker): I like to keep fit when I'm away, and so does John. We were away one day, I think we were in Wagga or Orange in country New South Wales, at one of our seminars, and John said to me, 'Wake me up in the morning and we'll go for a run.'

So I knocked on his door and he said, 'What have you been doing? You're late. I've already been for a run.'

I said, 'I want to go for a run now.'

So John said, 'I'll come again with you.'

We went down the street, and it was amazing for me to see people's reactions as they saw him. There were a lot of people who were stunned, they had never seen someone like John before, but there were also a lot of people who were like, 'Hey, how ya goin' mate? Have a great day.'

My job was to run in front of him and turn around and make sure there were no cars coming so he didn't get run over on the road because he was on his skateboard. At one point I said, 'Yep, the road's clear,' and all of a sudden a car came around the corner. I screamed, *'Stop!'* and at that second he put his hands on the ground on the bitumen, and I think he wore holes in his gloves because he stopped so quick.

When we turned to go home, the run was downhill at first, then we realised we had to go back *uphill!* Which was a really hard slog for him, as it was for me. I turned around and said to John, 'Gee my legs are hurting. Can we walk for a while?'

He said to me, 'I wish I had legs that could hurt.'

I said, 'Okay, I've got the message. Let's go.'

It was a really nice morning for me. It made me realise how lucky I am to have legs and how courageous John is to get out there and do the same things as everybody else.

Three Underrated Words

WHILE I WAS IN hospital recovering from that operation to remove my legs, I wrote down the things I wanted to do and the places where I wanted to go. The No. 1 thing on that list was to get my driver's licence.

I'd *always* wanted to drive a car. Or, to be more accurate, from the day my brother Adam got his licence and drove out of our driveway on his own, I knew I wanted to drive a car. It just seemed like *always*. 'If he can do it,' I told my Mum and Dad (and Adam), 'why can't I!'

I lay in that hospital, pen and paper in hand, and resolved to make that dream happen. The next time my Dad came to visit me, I told him resolutely that I wanted to get my L-plates pronto. 'Okay, that shouldn't be a problem,' he said. 'I'll ring the Motor Registry.'

I gave him a week to find out what we needed to do.

So Dad went away and within 24 hours he had the information we were after. 'Johnno,' he said flatly, 'it seems you can't drive a normal car.'

Duh! Good on yer, Dad.

'But once we find you a vehicle, and have it converted with hand controls, you'll be on your way,' he continued. 'All you've got to do is save up your money, then go and buy the car, and then go and get your driver's licence.'

Easy. I was working but not earning enough to buy that car. So I went and found another job. Fourteen months after that first conversation with my Dad, I went and bought my car, and later that day I went in and got my learner's permit.

When I proudly walked into my local Road and Traffic Authority (RTA) registry that day, the first thing I noticed was how high the counter was. From where I was, at the base of the counter, there was no way anyone was going to see me, let alone serve me. I was jumping up and down, yelling, 'I'm over here. Yoo-hoo, down here.' Eventually I dragged over a chair and leant up onto the counter, so at least my head, shoulders and chest were in view to those on the other side. I asked to be served, and a middle-aged woman came over.

'I'd like to apply for a licence, please,' I said.

'Certainly, sir,' she replied. 'I'll just get the paperwork.'

So far so good. Back she came. Soon we were filling out the relevant form – name, address, age, height, eye colour.

'Now,' she continued, 'do you wear glasses?'

'No, no, not at all. 20:20 vision,' I said a bit cheekily. I was all fired up, I wanted that licence.

'Do you have any other disabilities?'

Excuse me? Of course, she could hardly see below my chest. But I couldn't resist. I leapt on top of the counter. 'How about this?' I roared. Poor woman; it was so lucky there was a chair right behind her or she would have gone straight to the floor. If I'd had a video camera with me, I would have won 80 grand on the *Funniest Home Videos* TV show, just through the look on her face.

After the gobsmacked woman recovered her composure, and despite my behaviour, I got my licence.

And then I had to get some petrol. I pulled up at the station, and – wouldn't you know it – there was a very attractive lady filling her petrol tank. Like any single young bloke, I stared at her with a smile, and she looked back at me. And then, to really impress her, I wound the window down and jumped out of the car. She forgot what she was doing; petrol went everywhere. The door slammed shut; she was off, quick as a flash, without paying.

Looking back, this was cruel. But I was only trying to have some fun.

It was a special moment for me when I walked out of the RTA with that licence in my hand. For so long in my life I had been left far behind everybody else; even walking down the street I was always lagging 20 or 30 paces. I was the last person to walk through the restaurant door. I was even the last person to know when it was raining (though I was the first person to know when someone had farted). I'll never forget how I felt when I finally got behind that steering wheel. For the first time, I was able to keep up with everyone else.

Today, more than a decade after that momentous day when I became a licensed driver, I often get asked whether I can drive, how I do it, what kind of car I have. But the number of questions I get about my motoring skills is minuscule compared to the mountain of queries I receive concerning my relationships. It's as if people think that because I have such an obvious disability I'm unable to be in *any* kind of relationship. But I don't mind, because I have a great many close friendships that I love talking about. Some of the questions I hear are a bit strange, perhaps reflecting the insecurities of people.

'Do you have friends?'

'Why do you have relationships?'

'What do they mean?'

'What does the word "love" mean to you?'

'Who do you say it to?'

When I was invited to begin my public speaking career,

I had to think seriously about what I was going to say. I knew that my physical make-up would make an impact as soon as I walked out from behind the curtain, but that would be useless if I couldn't follow up with a worthwhile message. I needed to be much more than a 'freak' show. My speaking career would be a short one if I had nothing to say.

I felt that I did have something to say. The first 20 to 25 years of my life taught me so many things. Good and bad. I had learnt some valuable lessons about the importance of love. On one level, my story is that of a bloke who's made something of his life despite plenty of people doubting he could do so. On another, more powerful level, it is a 'love story', a tale of a bloke who made something of his life because a lot of people – including, most importantly, himself – believed he could.

'Love' is a word that means so much to so many people. Yet it is often hard for us to say. For some, strangely, it means absolutely nothing. These people can blurt out 'I love you' at the drop of a hat but never mean it. To me, those three very simple words, 'I love you', are both over-rated and extremely underrated.

Confused? Don't be.

It's just that they mean so much if they're from the heart but so little if used as a throwaway line. I tell my Mum and Dad more times than often that I love them. I tell my wife every day that I love her. I tell a whole variety of friends and family that I love them. Why? What's the motive behind it? Why is it important? Because these words mean a lot to me. The people that I say them to are really special to me.

Of all the times I told Mum and Dad I loved them, the one that has stayed with me the most was when I went in to have my legs amputated. Geez, I was only 18, an age when you don't say too much to your parents at all. Remember that part of your teenage years when you hate even spending time with your parents because they are *so* daggy? Later on, into your mid-twenties, you suddenly love spending time with them again. Anyway, I'm 18 and I'm trying to express my love for my parents just before I go in to have my legs amputated. 'Mum, Dad . . . I love you.'

And Dad says simply, 'I know son, that's good. I love you, too.'

Dad had said that to me before, but this time was different. It meant the world to me. I wasn't exactly sure what life had in store for me when I came out of that surgery but I knew I had the love of a wonderful father on my side. That's a powerful force to have in your corner.

But, of course, Mum and Dad weren't just backing me, they were backing my brothers and sister, too. Today, I reckon my parents have much to be proud of for the way they raised their kids and what's become of us.

Adam is into his mid-thirties, with a beautiful wife, Leonie, and three equally beautiful young kids, Kimberley, Amanda and little Harrison, aka 'Hurricane Harry'. They're living in a country town, a couple of hours' drive from Kalgoorlie in Western Australia, a little place that's home to around 650 adults and something like 300 kids.

Adam and Leonie left Sydney because they wanted a change. He's a cabinet-maker by trade and was a Rugby League hooker by sport, but now he's over there pig farming and loving every minute of it.

When Adam played footy he used to wear the old 'Benny Elias' headband – wads of duct tape wrapped around his melon to pin his ears back, so he wouldn't get those awful cauliflowered ears that many old forwards suffer through their ears rubbing on the legs and backsides of fellow forwards. It's funny. As well as the fact that he wasn't a bad player, the two things I remember about Adam Coutis on the footy field were his headband and his legs. God, he had bad legs. I mean, I know my legs weren't too flash, but his were shockers!

Sorry, brother!

Looking back, perhaps Adam was a little resentful that I took a lot of the attention from him, in the sense that because I needed so much from Mum and Dad, they didn't have enough time, in his eyes, for him. I have to stress that I'm talking about perceptions here, because I know my parents cared for him every bit as much as they cared for Luke, Kristy and me. My younger brother and sister didn't know any differently – from day one they were treated the way they were treated and I was treated the way I was treated – but maybe once or twice Adam got a little dirty at being second choice on the cab rank. I don't blame him for that; I mean, any normal kid would feel that way.

We used to fight like normal kids, too. But I was always his little brother, and watch out anyone who would ever say a hurtful thing about me. It was all right for him to say bad things about me, but if anybody else stepped inside that circle, well, they needed to be careful. Through the 1990s, whether Adam was living in our family home in North Richmond, or in his own house in the area, or whether he and his family were far away on the other side of the country, we kept that bond. Luke was the same. He was always there for me when I needed him. And me for him.

Like me, Adam and Luke both worked at Dad's factory, and the place offered a terrific grounding for the three of us. At that time, the Coutis clan seemed entrenched in the Richmond area, but nowadays Kristy is the only one of us still living there. She's working at the local hospital and not married yet, though somehow I think that might be her brothers' fault. In the early 1990s, when guys would come to the front door to take her out, we three brothers – Stooges, Amigos, call us what you like – would rush out and answer the door before she could get there.

'Mate,' we'd ask straightaway and straight-faced to her latest suitor, 'have you got any money?'

'Nah, not a lot,' might be the reply.

And we'd slam the door.

Or we'd ask, 'What kind of car do you drive?'

'A Holden,' Kristy's date would reply, pointing out at a Holden panel van parked in front of our house.

'Sorry, no panel vans,' we'd shriek, and the door would be slammed again.

And then, when these poor guys finally got past us, they

had to introduce themselves to Dad, a big marshmallow of a man who looked for all the world like a character from the *Sopranos* or the *Godfather* movies.

Today, my parents are based on the New South Wales north coast, about halfway between Sydney and Brisbane. Happily away from the hustle and bustle of the city, they chose that area because they'd been going up that way for holidays for the best part of 30 years and just love it. As do I. Mum's still doing a bit of nursing, and Dad works as a foreman, still making a buck but away from the tools that were so much a part of his working life for so long.

Friendship is something that many people take for granted, and don't realise how special it is until it's taken away from them. I'll always miss Matthew Anderson, my best friend. He was such a trooper, always positive. He had suffered from an accident at his birth, when he was mishandled and left with a severely damaged spine. But forget the disabilities, in other ways we were even more alike – both 'sick-witted', quick to crack silly, sometimes outrageous jokes. I called him 'Virgil' because, like the fella from the *Thunderbirds*, he was so all out of shape. But he was a qualified disc jockey and successful radio announcer, with a brain that clicked 24–7, as in 24 hours a day, seven days a week. He came up with some of the most fantastic jingles I've ever heard. Or ever will hear.

He once told me that if I ever wrote a book I had to call it *From the Ground Up*.

We were so close I called his parents Mum and Dad, as he did with mine. Matthew was at me for years and years to move in together and at 26 I decided to take the plunge. It was at least in part to show my parents that no one would need to worry about me when they'd gone, and to prove to myself that I'd be okay.

So we moved into a house. The date was 16 June 1996. What an experience! Little things. Just to be able to select *our* furniture, and the kitchenware and everything else and then to be able to put it where *we* wanted it. To show people *our* house. Fantastic! To host our parties, play loud music late at night, come home late and try to put our keys in the lock of our front door. And then, on 26 June, Matthew passed away. He just died in his sleep. Gone.

I still live in that house. My memories of Matthew remain within these four walls. But there were no 'I love you's' when he left, no 'goodnights', it was all so sudden. All it was, was ten days of bliss. We moved in on 16 June, and he died ten days later, just didn't get up in the morning. Just did not wake up. We'd both taken it for granted.

'See you in the morning, buddy.'

'No problems, champ. See you then. Have a good night's sleep.'

The bastard, he's still sleeping.

I remember Matthew's death as if it happened yesterday – how I was up there on top of him, belting his chest, trying mouth-to-mouth. Please, mate, *wake up*! I didn't know how long he'd been lying there so still, his lips blue, the back of his neck cold.

What had happened was so simple, yet so totally, cruelly unexpected. His spine had been bent out of shape since birth, and as he got older, while he was never in any pain (you know, he hardly ever got sick), his spine had nowhere to grow. It couldn't grow straight, so it grew into his body and gradually squashed his heart and his lungs against his rib cage. Then one night, just like that, it was too much. No one knew that he had a terminal disability. Looking back on my time living with Matthew, nothing we could have done would have changed anything about the sudden way it ended. We had ten great days.

I often wonder whether his mum and stepdad would have raised him any differently had they known that he was going to die when he got to his mid- to late-twenties. I hope not and I doubt it. Because we had a great life together – some of the things we used to get up to – had such a great time. We were absolute terrors.

One hilarious incident that happened long before we moved in together is locked firmly in my memory. It occurred when we travelled to Brisbane for a wheelchair footy State of Origin match. Matthew often struggled to get up and down escalators on his own in his electric wheelchair. We were in Surfers Paradise on the Gold Coast when he came upon a really long travelator, like the ones you see at airports, only this one took you from one level to another and was on a pretty steep angle. Matthew didn't like the look of it one bit.

All the other kids in their electric wheelchairs got on and went down, no problem at all, but poor Matthew was scared shitless. I said, 'C'mon, mate, come on. You'll be right.' By now, everyone else in the group was down the other end, but still my good friend wouldn't get on board. Finally, exasperated, I said, 'Look, mate, you're holding us up. I'll hold onto you.' To be honest, I was a little dirty, because I trusted him with my life and he did the same with me, so if I'd thought it was going to be too dangerous for him I would have said so, told him to go and get in the lift down the other end of the shopping centre. The way you do it is simple. You turn the electric wheelchair off and leave it turned off until you reach the bottom, when you turn it back on and just ride off. Easy.

Finally, he got on the travelator, and I'm on my skateboard in front of him. And that wheelchair of his is bloody heavy, and it was about now that I realised just how bloody steep this travelator is. About halfway down, the weight of the wheelchair knocked me off my skateboard. A bit further and I couldn't hold the chair any more, though I kept hold of my mate, determined that he wouldn't fall out of his seat. Down we went – me, Matthew and wheelchair, in that order, with the skateboard trailing behind. The last eight or so seconds of that ride was sheer terror, for him and me.

At the bottom there was a little rise, which we hit hard. At that point, Matthew turned his chair back on and shot out of the travelator. The problem with that was that I was still right in front of him, so he ran straight over the top of me. Then my skateboard went boom! straight into the back of my head. When the dust cleared, he was fine, all our colleagues were laughing themselves silly, I couldn't move. The physical hurt lasted a short time, the tyre marks eventually disappeared from my forehead, but my embarrassment lasted a whole while longer.

I took Matthew's death personally. Looking back it was the wrong thing to do, but that's how I reacted. I always thought I could take care of him, no matter what happened, that everything would be okay. When he died, I suddenly thought no, I can't take care of him. Christ, I'm lucky to take care of myself.

I started thinking, Is my disability terminal?

Am I helpless?

And from that, When am I going to die?

I went to my doctor and asked these questions and many others. There was nothing the matter with me. Nothing. When I asked my Dad he gave me the same answer he'd always given me, the same answer he'd have given my brothers and sister, if they'd have asked him.

'Dad, am I going to die?'

'Yes, son. We all are.'

Part of a Team

ONE OF MY CLOSEST friends is Stephen Waugh. I met Stephen around ten years ago, at a pub out at Richmond, at a time when he'd already been an international sportsman for four or five years. He was out west preparing for a pre-season match involving the New South Wales Sheffield Shield squad.

Steve Waugh: It was the night before the trial game, and we were having a couple of drinks, playing a little pool, basically relaxing out the back of the pub, and I saw ... well, I didn't know what it was at first ... I saw this person scampering along the ground, then hopping up on a chair, then a bar stool and then straight up onto the bar. That caught my eye. I didn't know what was going on. Then I saw this guy hop down off the bar, the stool and the chair, and scurry off with a couple of drinks back to his mates.

I did a double take, and then I went over to him to have a bit of a chat.

As I remember it, part of my initial conversation with Stephen went like this:

Steve Waugh: Do you like cricket?

Me: Bloody oath, mate! I love it!

Steve Waugh: Well, why don't you pop down to Benson's Lane [the ground where the trial match was scheduled to be played] and you can have a bit of a field for us.

Me: What time do you start?

Next morning I was the first person at the ground, all dressed in my whites with my Dad laughing, 'You're a bloody idiot, son. They're not gonna let you field.' I quietly reintroduced myself to Steve and then stayed out of trouble until, while the members of the squad were completing their preparations before the start of play, I sneaked into the dressing room and hid in one of the bloke's 'coffins' (large kitbags). When the players returned to the dressing room, I waited until they were all sitting quietly and then I bounced out like a jack-in-the-box, scaring the shit out of one or two of the young blokes sitting nearby. From that moment, I was 'in' in the team.

A little later on, I walked out onto Benson's Lane, alongside Stephen and wearing a pair of sunnies and the blue helmet the guys had given me to field in. At the gate was a little fella, no more than six or seven years old, who looked at his hero, Steve Waugh, then looked down at me, looked at his Dad standing there, looked down at me again, and then shrieked, 'Look, Dad. A walking helmet!'

That brought me back down to earth. Still, I stayed out there for a long time and sledged the blokes from the other team every chance I got.

> **Steve Waugh:** He fielded at short leg for my side, and fielded magnificently, stopping quite a few balls. He also sledged [NSW wicketkeeper] Phil Emery when Phil got out, caught down the leg side – gave him a real gobful. Johnno stayed on for about 15 overs; in the end we couldn't get rid of him. We wanted to sub him for one of the authentic players, but initially he refused to go. He certainly made his mark.

I developed a kinship not only with Stephen but also with the Bankstown Cricket Club, of which he has been a renowned member for so long. On quite a few occasions he has taken me over to watch the team play, and I now consider myself a good friend of the Bankstown club and the entire Waugh family. I was very grateful for the care and kindness of Stephen's Mum, Bev, who became like a second mother to me. I also became great mates with

Stephen's brother, Dean, who's my age and like me is something of a lunatic. Dean's living in Adelaide now, but back in the good old days we had some bloody great times together. There were a number of times when I managed to field close-in for Bankstown for a couple of overs, another fantastic credit to put on my résumé.

Gavin Robertson: During the 1992–93 season, I got thrown into the NSW team. That was the year the 'Baby Blues' won nine or ten games in a row to win everything. 'JC' was coming to the cricket with me every day, and our friendship grew from there.

That season we won the Mercantile Mutual Cup, and John said that he was my driver for the night. I set him up on a table with the trophy. Everyone on the team drank all night; it ended up being this big night out together. I remember coming home really late, 4.30 am, and for some reason my parents were still up. My uncle and auntie were also there. I introduced John, and they didn't know what was going on. They said, 'How're you going?' and he said, 'I'm great and I've had a great night. Geez, life's good.' I just love the fact that he was as natural with them as he is with me.

That's the thing about him. I don't think of John as having no legs. When you first meet him you wouldn't think you'd ever get to that stage. Actually, this conversation now is probably the first time since I met him that I've thought about the fact that he's got no legs.

During the 1993–94 Australian summer, I was invited by Stephen to watch a Test match between Australia and

South Africa at the Sydney Cricket Ground. Before the game I was invited to go onto the field and warm up with the team and give the guys a bit of a pep talk. Afterwards I was allowed into the home team's dressing room. There I met a few stars from the cricket and entertainment worlds, including the Australian captain, the great Allan Border, plus the music guru Molly Meldrum. I also met John Cornell and Austin Robertson, two of the principal figures in the development of World Series Cricket, the revolution that so changed the game in the late 1970s. John Cornell is also very famous for being Paul Hogan's sidekick, 'Strop', on *The Paul Hogan Show*.

When I was introduced to John and Austin, they asked me if I was really keen on cricket. 'Oh, yes,' I blurted out. 'I love it!'

'You know the team is about to leave for South Africa?' John then said. 'Would you like to go with them?'

'Well, yeah, I'd love to go,' I said. 'But, mate, there's no way I could afford the fare.'

'Just leave that with me,' was all John Cornell said.

I didn't get my hopes up because even well-meaning people say things to you that they don't always follow through. In this case, I'd known John Cornell for a bit less than five minutes. But, sure enough, about a week later I had a phone call from Austin Robertson.

'Johnno,' he began, 'we've organised it with the Australian Cricket Board and we're going to pay your way for you to go to South Africa.'

And all I could say was, 'Shit, you are kidding me!'

I couldn't believe what I'd just heard. 'It's all paid for, everything's done,' Austin explained, and I said 'Thank you very much' about a thousand times.

When that phone conversation ended, I sat by the phone for ages, unable to take in what had just happened to me. John Coutis from North Richmond was about to go on tour with the Australian cricket team, was about to share hotel rooms with Allan Border, Ian Healy, David Boon, Stephen Waugh, Shane Warne, Merv Hughes, Mark Taylor, Craig McDermott, Mark Waugh, Glenn McGrath, Dean Jones, Michael Slater – unbelievable.

Closer to my departure day, I began to worry that I was going to be seen as some form of 'fuzzy wuzzy' mascot for the side. But the boys gave me the title of assistant physio and team trainer, which I appreciated. In truth, I was more of a 'gofer' in the dressing room and at training, fetching balls and equipment, answering whatever request might be thrown my way. I truly didn't care what the boys wanted, I'd have done it. I was so honoured to be there and kept reminding myself that there were literally tens of thousands of people who would have loved to have been in my position. I'd like to think that I gave the team something in return, perhaps a little bit of inspiration.

On that tour I learnt how much fun it is to be an international cricketer, and how gruelling it is. I never realised just how much hard bloody work those blokes put in to be able to compete and remain at that level. It's not just working your butt off to make it; once you're there, that's when the serious work begins. I also learnt how incredibly gifted these Test cricketers are. Their talent is so much greater than anything I ever saw out at Richmond or Windsor cricket grounds.

I know how hard Australia's premier wheelchair athlete, Louise Sauvage, trains to stay at the elite level in her sport, to win so many world titles and have all the world records that are attached to her belt. I know, too, how seriously Stephen Waugh trains to stay at the top of the cricket tree. My trip to South Africa, like my own participation in elite-level sport, showed me that if I want to be successful at anything, sport or otherwise, then I need to put the work in. As Australia's greatest sporting and business achievers have demonstrated, it's never going to come easily, but if you want it badly enough, you can reach your goals.

The tour was full of memorable moments. I was there in Durban for the third Test when Allan Border faced his last ball in Test cricket. It was the end of an era, one of the greatest cricketers of all time playing his final hand. But what I remember most was the way the South African public always wanted a piece of the Australian players. They'd walk down the street and everybody would want to talk to them, get them to sign autographs, pose for a photograph, talk some more. Even I got to sign autographs! No one knew who the hell I was, but I was with the Australian cricket side so I had to be important. In truth, I felt pretty out of place but I was having so much fun I hardly ever stopped to think about that.

Steve Waugh: At the beach in Durban, the kids would see him almost every day – they'd be riding their skateboards down the promenade and John would be riding his. A couple of times, they asked what had happened to him and he said, 'Just make sure you don't go in the water with the sharks around.'

One mistake I made was to try to keep up with these professional sportsmen in the drinking stakes. When will I ever learn? One night, Big Merv let me sleep in the drawer of a cupboard in his hotel room, where I happily dozed off the effects of one too many lagers.

One of the funniest things to happen to me – and among the most embarrassing stories involving John Coutis ever – occurred on this tour. We pulled into Johannesburg on a very hot day, around 38 degrees with extreme humidity, and by the time we checked into our hotel I was dying for a drink. Any drink. The mini-bar was locked. There were taps and glasses in the bathroom, but I couldn't reach them from ground level, and no matter how I looked at it, I couldn't work out a way to climb up onto the washbasin. My mouth was so dry, I was desperate, and then salvation caught my eye. But what it was, I had no idea.

You have to remember that I was raised in what was, to all intents and purposes, a small country town. This was the first flash hotel I'd ever stayed in. Next to the toilet was a contraption, the like of which I'd never seen in my life. No, that's not true. I'd actually seen them many times, in schoolyards, in parks, on golf courses. It was a water-bubbler. At the height it was at, about knee level for an adult, it was a kid's bubbler. What it was doing next to the loo, I had no idea. Not very hygienic but, hey, I was just grateful that it was there.

I pushed the 'button' next to this thing and, like magic, water spouted out. You beauty, except, I suddenly thought, how the hell am I going to get my mouth up to the spout? I put one hand on the button up on the wall and the other flat on the ground. Then I positioned myself at a perfect 180-degree angle, arms and lips outstretched, pushed the button with my 'top' hand, and merrily drank away. It was so refreshing, a little bit minty to taste maybe, but just what I needed. Then the porter entered the room with my bags.

'Mate, I'm in here having a drink. Just drop 'em anywhere you like,' I called out.

Through the open door, he saw me slurping away.

'*Whhhaaaattttt* are you doing?' he screamed as the bags dropped to the floor. 'No, no, no, that is not for drinking.'

'Whaddya mean not for drinking?' I responded. 'What else could it be for?'

And, very slowly, the porter explained what I should have been using it for. The first time, he put things fairly delicately, and I didn't catch on. 'Mate, speak English,' I pleaded, perhaps a tad angrily.

'Look, sir, it's called a bidet,' he shot back. 'You use the toilet, then you hop on there, push the button, and the water cleans your bum.'

'Oh, shit!' I yelled out. '*Yuukkkk!* I'm gonna die, I've been drinking toilet water.'

My reaction was so spontaneous, loud and revolting that a couple of the Test stars rushed in to see what was wrong. I was about to say, 'No, nothin', don't worry,' when this bloody porter blurted out the whole story. My shame was complete. By the time I entered the bar soon after, my drinking habits were the talk of the team, the bar, and, it seemed, the whole bloody city. There was nothing I could do but try to laugh it off. It was one way to learn.

Mum, if you want to know what it tastes like, it's just like your Earl Grey tea.

At the end of the tour the squad split up, with a couple going to England, many jetting off to another tour, to Sharjah in the United Arab Emirates, and the remainder (including me) heading home. I had the pleasure of sitting next to Merv Hughes on that homeward trip, and swapping yarns with champions such as Dean Jones, Allan Border and Ian Healy.

During that flight, we had to put up with a flight attendant who had clearly come on board in a very bad mood. Wherever I go, whether it be Burwood, Bourke or Brussels, I always try to put smiles on people's faces. All I wanted to do was turn that lady's frown upside down, but I didn't know how to go about it.

So I said to the boys, 'Look, we need to try to work out a way to make this girl smile and feel good about herself. Let's put our thinking caps on and see what we can come up with.'

We regrouped after a few minutes, but no one had any inspiration. 'Heals' couldn't think of anything. 'AB', nothing.

'Deano' – he had some ideas, but nothing of substance. Merv, meanwhile, was sitting there saying nothing, but moving his hands about as if he was measuring me for a suit fitting. What the hell is he doing, I wondered.

All of a sudden, the big fella jumped up and took the pillows out of the overhead locker. Uh, oh! Then he picked me up and threw me inside. Unfortunately Merv's measurements weren't 100 per cent, and I didn't quite fit in, but a small matter like that wasn't going to stop him and he squeezed me in like Steve Waugh trying to fit all his cricket gear into his kitbag. I was crammed in there like a whale in a sardine can, and then the locker door slammed pitch-black shut. He'll only leave me in for a minute, I thought. Won't he? After ten minutes I was starting to worry about whether lack of oxygen might be a problem, when we crashed into a bit of turbulence. Down below, I heard that bitter and twisted hostie talking to Merv.

'Mr Hughes, where's Mr Coutis?' she said sternly. 'Why isn't he in his seat?'

'Nah, don't worry,' Big Merv replied politely. 'He's in the gents, he won't be long.'

'Well, I'm sorry, the seat-belt sign is on. Mr Coutis should be in his seat. Please tell him to stay in his seat.'

'Certainly, I am sorry,' Merv continued. 'And if it's not too much trouble, I can't get up, would you mind grabbing me a pillow, please.'

Now I knew what was happening. I sensed the hostess's hand reaching up to my locker, and when the door opened I rolled out, straight on top of her. The poor woman almost had a heart attack. She fell back onto Merv, and I fell on her, and everyone around us burst out laughing. Fortunately, she saw the funny side of it. When we bumped into her on the way out after we landed, she stepped forward, gave me a kiss on the forehead and apologised for having been in such a bad mood. I gave her my standard reply, 'You don't have to apologise; everybody has bad days. You just need to take what you have and do what you can with it every single day.'

Wayne Pearce, the great Rugby League back-row forward, was one of my heroes when I was growing up. Wayne played for the mighty Balmain Tigers, and while I was not a Tigers supporter, I admired his dedication to physical fitness and his career, and appreciated the way he always conducted himself professionally and with great dignity. One day in the late 1980s, I sat down and wrote a letter to Wayne, addressed to the Balmain Leagues Club, asking if he would write a weightlifting program and a general fitness program for me. Which he promptly did.

This was my first direct link with the top figures in Australian Rugby League. Soon after, however, I found myself doing a bit of work with Geoff 'Jethro' Gerard at the Penrith Rugby League Club. He was coach of their President's Cup (under 21) team (and later the reserve-grade side), and had a big influence on my life for a couple of years. My job was to keep the stats, help out in the change rooms, even send messages out onto the field, and I did a good enough job in 1990 to get invited on the boys' end-of-season trip to Hawaii, my first overseas adventure. All the club's players were on that holiday except for the four internationals – John Cartwright, Greg Alexander, Brad Fittler and Mark Geyer – who were in England with the Australian team. This was the year the first-grade team reached the grand final for the first time, and all three grades reached the semis. It was also the first time I had travelled anywhere without my Mum and Dad.

I really learnt a lot about myself in Hawaii. I'd just turned 21, and unless you're 21 in the US you can't do many things that I discovered were compulsory on end-of-season trips. Geez, I saw a lot of pubs and bars while I was there.

I'm a Penrith boy through and through. I love the mighty Penrith Panthers and love all the guys who play for them but I'll never forgive them for a couple of shocking experiences with alcohol that I had while I was in the US's fiftieth state. Like any newcomer on tour, I was eager to impress, but when it came to the demon drink I didn't have anything like the stamina of these hardened professionals.

One night on that trip, I got myself terribly drunk and had a helluva journey, not long before sunrise, stumbling back to my room. I have got to tell you that not having any legs gives 'stumbling back to my room' a whole new meaning. It was all I could do to take off my clothes and collapse on my bed. It wasn't until 2 pm that I woke, in an awful sweat with the sun beaming through the very large and open doors of my room. For hours, the hot Hawaiian sun had been roasting me, and my bum was now red raw sunburnt. My head was sore, my throat was dry, the gut was very unstable and because of the blisters that soon emerged on my butt, I couldn't sit down for weeks. This remains my worst hangover of all time. Some of life's lessons are very simple. If you're going to fall asleep drunk, get under the blankets.

Don't forget it. I never have.

Going overseas and experiencing places that I'd only previously seen in tourist brochures really opened my eyes to the fact that there were other cultures beyond North Richmond. I had a great time over there in Hawaii, a great time.

I must confess that when I was offered a spot on that tour I saw it as the chance to express my growing self-reliance by being away from Mum and Dad. Yet, inevitably, I was also apprehensive. I craved independence and at the same time was afraid of it. So this trip was very important for me. In the days leading up to our departure, my head kept suggesting I should put it off, maybe go next year. But my heart knew it was the right time to go. And there was not one moment in Hawaii when I didn't want to be there.

I arrived home on my parents' wedding anniversary, 16 October. And looking back, I was probably a little bit too cocky for my own good when I returned. After all, I now knew every pick-up line ever invented (even if they didn't work for me), and was aware that putting beer on your cornflakes was perfectly logical. For a day or two, I kept reminding Mum and Dad that I was now a seasoned international adventurer, but the Old Man kicked that arrogance out of me quick smart.

Wayne Pearce had retired as a player at the end of that 1990 season, but in 1994 he took over as coach of the Tigers and in 1999 was coach of the New South Wales State of Origin side as well. One day while he was in camp with the NSW Blues, he called to invite me to give a motivational talk to his players. What an honour! Of course, I jumped at the chance, but then I thought, What am I going to say?

When I first found myself in a dressing room with all these great footballers, I was unbelievably nervous. The Coutis name had been synonymous with local League in the Richmond area, and both my brothers were good footy players. Back in the 1980s, if you'd framed a market as to which of the Coutis boys would turn up in a State of Origin dressing room, I think you would have got pretty long odds about the shortest of us. Yet here I was shaking hands with champions such as Laurie Daley and Brad Fittler. And still the thought was nagging at me, What to say? I mean, there was no point telling the tough and brilliant halfback Andrew Johns to never give up. Or to tell the proud and brave front rower Mark 'Spud' Carroll to go out there and be himself. In the end, I shared with them some of my life stories, many of the stories that are in this book, and hoped that the guys might draw something from them, each in a different way.

When the Blues won the second game, in Sydney, I was

in the dressing room afterwards. Without a hint of a warning, Spud picked me up and carried me into the celebratory huddle, one of my most special moments ever. All of my life, I'd wanted to play Rugby League, to be good at it. Of course, it was a dream that was never going to come true; the closest I'd ever come was those games in the backyard at my grandmother's place with all my cousins and my two brothers, when I often ended up being used as the ball. To be in this huddle, feeling as if I'd contributed in some small way to the victory, was as good as it gets.

I've played many different sports on many different fields. But my biggest achievement is not some game I won, or weight I lifted, or run I scored, or team I led. My greatest feat, in my opinion, is that every time I have taken part in competitive sport, I have given it 120 per cent. If I can't give 120 per cent then I won't bother. If I win after giving it my all, then that's a bonus.

I've played against guys with much more severe disabilities than me. Mostly, the disability that's beaten them has been their attitude. I'd like to think I might have shown a few of them a better way to get things done.

I honestly believe that if it wasn't for sport I wouldn't be here today. Sport has helped me through so many difficulties in my life, and it's provided me with heaps of challenges, too. It's also taught me a helluva lot about myself.

My sporting life has shown me how to deal with ups and downs, and it has taught me the value of the three Ds. Through sport I know the importance of self-discipline, desire and being dedicated to the cause. These days, without sport in my life, I sometimes long for an opportunity to come into contact again with those three aspects of sporting preparation. Similarly with the three Ps that are so much a part of sport – perseverance, pain and pride. I know now that we need to have these three critters in every walk of life, but it was in sport that I first appreciated their value.

I was in the athletes' village the night Cathy Freeman won her gold medal at the Sydney Olympics in September 2000. The night was, of course, such a wonderful one for Cathy, Australia and Australian sport, but one small negative for me was when the PM came up to me early on, patted me on the head and said, 'How are you goin', little fella?' It was so degrading; clearly he assumed that because I was physically disabled I was mentally retarded as well. It reflected the way many parts of the community still have much to learn about the disabled. Perhaps foolishly, just as I did when I was treated this way by unenlightened adults when I was a kid, I acted as if I was mentally retarded, to make my point. Then I quickly regained my composure and responded, 'I'm sorry. I'm all right, thanks.' Just as quickly, Mr Howard apologised, which is to his credit, and then he was on his way.

The Paralympics that followed the Olympics were fantastic, though on a personal level I found the experience frustrating because I had so desperately wanted to be a part of it – on the field.

To be honest, I was also a little annoyed by the way the media and the public were *so* ultra-positive, to the point that no one was game to be even remotely critical. These were elite athletes, and some performed below expectations, a fact that in my view should have been pointed out but wasn't. For example, I went to the gold medal match for the quad Rugby, a sport I love because it's the only genuine contact sport in the Olympics or the Paralympics, besides wrestling, boxing and taekwondo. It's a smash 'em, knock 'em-out-of-their-chairs sport; if you fall out of your wheelchair and you're in the way, then you'll be wearing tyre treadmarks. The Yanks were winning, and the Aussies had the ball until one of our blokes threw it over the top to a teammate, but the pass was dropped. It shouldn't have been. Everyone went, 'Ohhh, what a shame.' Everyone except me. I yelled out, 'You're supposed to catch it, *you idiot*!' Eight thousand eyes stared straight in the direction of that remark, then they saw me and everyone started laughing. I don't think too many other people could have got away with such a remark. But I was there as a fan, and they were my feelings, and he should have caught the bloody thing. I know that if a champion such as Laurie Daley or Brad Fittler had spilt that ball in a Rugby League grand final when they were about to score a try, everyone would have hammered him. But when I made my outburst, the reaction was, 'You can't do that.' You can and you should.

I couldn't help thinking at times during the Paralympics, as I watched different events, I wanted that so much to be me. I don't usually think in terms of 'could haves', 'maybes' and 'probablys', but you must understand that I didn't retire from the sport, my chance was taken away from me by illness. Speak to any athlete and they'll tell you that there's a bloody big difference between retiring and having your opportunity taken away from you because of injuries, ill health or whatever.

In fact, I couldn't even go to the early days of the Paralympics. I had a series of presentations to do for schools on the New South Wales north coast, although I could just as easily have drawn a line through my diary to keep the ten days free for me to go to the Games. I did end up going to a number of events, and having a terrific time, but in the early days it was hard.

I actually watched the opening ceremony at my parents' house up north. I was sitting there watching Karen Tighe, the female equivalent of Bruce McAvaney, hosting ABC's television coverage, and I could feel the tears welling up. This was what I had wanted to do, to walk out there as part of the Aussie squad. I had to turn it off and go to bed.

My feelings were the same later, when I watched the weightlifting. I kept thinking it could have been me. I have to stress that while my lifting was really coming on until illness wrecked my preparation, I was no good thing to make the Aussie team. I would have needed to put in a helluva lot of work to get there, but I had the determination to do that work. At the Paralympics, the winning lift in what would have been my weight division was 168kg, which is more than 40kg heavier than I have ever lifted. But my goal, which I set myself two years before the Games, was to be lifting 180kg by 2000. I know that's huge, but that was my goal. Whether I could have done it, we'll never know.

I didn't go to the athletes' village for the Paralympics. I didn't want to – not out of spite or bitterness, just disappointment. For the Olympics, that was different; I jumped at the chance to mix with some of the Aussie team. If I hadn't been a Paralympic athlete who wasn't competing in Sydney, had I merely been a sports fan, I reckon I would have jumped just as quickly at the chance to go to the Paralympic Village. In my eyes, the guys in that village were every bit as important and skilful as the Olympians. But, as I said, my situation was different. I hope people understand that.

Kids for Life

THERE I WAS IN the supermarket. My shopping trolley and I were in the cereal aisle, where I walked over to the second-from-bottom shelf and grabbed a pack of cornflakes or whatever it was that was my fancy that week. I lobbed it into my trolley, then walked a bit further down the aisle and climbed up the shelves to grab something else. I was about to pick out another of life's essentials when I noticed a little boy in the next aisle who was staring at me through the gaps between products on the shelves. I quickly caught on that he thought I was the funniest, most unusual, most intriguing thing he'd ever seen in his life. When he realised that I'd spotted him looking at me, he yelled out, 'Mum, Mum. Hey, Mum, have a look. It's a monkey! It's a monkey!'

Mum, of course, was appalled and embarrassed. She grabbed her son by the arm and whispered loudly (which is possible under these circumstances), 'Shussh! *Shusshh!*' She might have even given him a whack on the backside.

I love watching kids. Often, I get a kick out of watching the reactions of parents to their kids, too. In this case, the poor woman didn't know what to do, while all her little boy wanted to know was what it was that he had just seen. Quickly, the woman remembered she needed something from many aisles away, but within minutes her son had got away from her and was back checking me out once more.

At the end of one of the aisles, this little bloke came right up close to me and stood there, looking at me. His poor mother rushed up, shaking in her boots, thinking, no doubt, What's going to happen here? Finally, my inquisitive little mate said something.

'What 'appened to you?'

Now I was on the spot. What did happen to me? I had to think about that. His Mum heard him ask and said something along the lines of, 'Holy shit!'

I looked straight and hard at her son and said to him, 'Mate, at dinner time, when I was a little boy like you, I didn't eat all my vegetables. Then my legs got really really sick and the doctor had to take them away.'

The thing I'll never forget was the look on the face of the mother. She went from being so embarrassed to giving me one of the biggest and warmest smiles I'd ever received. I grinned back at her. The little boy, meanwhile, was taking the news in. It certainly wasn't what he'd been expecting. He, I'm sure, was expecting a tale about a shark attack, or some other ghastly accident.

Fifteen minutes later I had finished my shopping and took my trolley to the checkout. As I placed my groceries on the counter, I looked up to see, three or four aisles away, my new friends doing the same. And the little bloke? He was feverishly chewing at a piece of frozen broccoli!

Maybe what I said wasn't the right thing to say. Maybe it was. I'm no expert. But it was what I decided to say under a bit of pressure, and I know it made me feel good, it made his mother feel good, and it most certainly made this little boy think. Hopefully, it also meant that he'll be eating his vegies for the rest of his life. Most importantly, I reckon the interaction we had would have helped break down the barrier between so-called 'able' and 'disabled' people, at least in the minds of this mother and son.

Kath Robertson (Gavin's wife): I remember when our daughter Zoe was in the high chair and John walked in – sorry, toddled in – to our house on his hands. He chuckled, 'I've left my shoes at the door.' Then he walked around the corner, Zoe turned around and, all of eight months old, she just goes, 'Aaahhhh!' This freakish scream came out of her mouth as if to say, 'My God, what is that?' We all looked at each other and burst out laughing, which you can do with John, whereas a lot of other people in John's position would have said, 'I'm sorry for upsetting your child.' He straightaway started laughing about it and thought, Okay, now I'm going to play another joke on someone else.

One of the better pranks I ever played was sparked by my feelings about kids. It occurred while I was in Hawaii with the Penrith Rugby League boys in 1990 – the trip where I got that terrible sunburn. Maybe it was a bit cruel, but I don't care. It remains a favourite memory of my time there. One sunny day on Waikiki Beach, I was sitting under a palm tree watching some little kids, they were not much more than babies, playing in the sand. They were having the time of their lives, digging into the beach, building sandcastles and splashing in the water while their parents chatted among themselves, not too far away. It was one of those simple moments that reminds you just how much fun it is to be a child.

It fascinated me to see these kids making plenty out of nothing. They were architects, they were construction workers, they were contractors, they were supervisors – you name it, they were it – crafting their sandcastles. In short, they were having a ball, and at the same time showing others on the beach how to have fun.

Then along came Scrooge, in the form of a group of young 'adults', about 17, 18 or 19 years old. Stupid bastards; it was too much trouble to walk around the sandcastles, so they just kicked them over. Sand went flying into the water, and then to exacerbate their crime they grabbed the kids' buckets and shovels and threw them in the water. The poor children, who not two minutes earlier had being building their dream castles, had had their party ruined by the boofheads and their angry attitudes. They went screaming back to their parents, their tears just about the worst sound you'll ever hear in your life, if you ask me. And their assailants continued their arrogant stroll along the beach, their swagger and ridiculous high fives suggesting (to themselves at least) that they were heroes. They weren't heroes to me.

I thought to myself, If you were on any beach in Australia, any beach whatsoever, you wouldn't get away with that. You certainly wouldn't have got away with it on the riverbank at North Richmond. If only some of my tourmates from the Panthers had been there. But here, it seemed no one was going to do anything to right this injustice. So I took it upon myself to stand up for these kids. When I saw that these arrogant bastards were on their way back towards us, I jumped up and took myself down to where those fabulous sandcastles had once proudly stood. There, near the water's edge, while the kids and their parents watched, I dug a little hole – it didn't have to be a real big hole, did it? – sat myself in there, dragged the sand back over the hole so it seemed I was buried to the waist, and waited for these blokes to return.

When they reached me, I looked up and said, 'G'day. How are you going?'

'Not bad, man,' one of them replied. 'Whatcha doin'?'

'Mate,' I said sternly, 'my mates have buried me here and left me. You reckon you could give me a lift to get out?'

'Yeah, mate,' they responded, mimicking my Aussie accent, 'not a problem.'

Mate, I was smiling inside. Two or three of them

grabbed my left arm, the others grabbed my right. I said, 'Okay. Right, now, one, two, three – pull as hard as you can.'

And pull hard they did. Out I popped, as easy as you like, but all these dopey blokes saw was nothing from the waist down. 'Oh, shit!' I screamed. 'What have you done?' They took one more look, dropped me flat and bolted like Carl Lewis at the Olympics. And they sure could run fast, let me tell you.

You don't always have to be big to throw a big punch. The little kids didn't know what was going on, but their parents did and so did I. Within seconds, the children were back at their construction site, rebuilding their dreams. Those gooses were still sprinting up the beach – it was one of the funniest things I've seen in my life.

To add to that punchline, one of the beautiful little kids then came up to me, put her arm around me, and said quietly, 'Don't worry, mister, we'll help you find your legs.' There was no point explaining that I didn't have any. She and a couple of her friends then starting digging and digging and digging, and would have gone all the way to China if I'd let them. Meanwhile, those boofheads were *still* running up the beach.

Why do I get on so well with children? One of the reasons is that I'm the same size as them. Seriously. To them, I'm just a kid with a deeper voice, plus I reckon they realise that I'm just a kid at heart.

One of the biggest differences between kids and adults is that the feedback I get from kids is *always* direct and honest. It doesn't matter what age they are, you know, from five to ten years old; kids don't care what people think, they just blurt it out and there it is.

I laugh so hard at some of the names the kids call me. I've been called an 'Oompa Loompa' after the characters from *Charlie and the Chocolate Factory*. I've been 'Uncle Half' (my all-time favourite), 'Kermit the Frog', 'Carrot Legs', 'Poppa Smurf'. I've been called all kinds of different things, but never once have I complained, because kids don't have a malicious bone in their bodies. As I sit here right now, I'm smiling at the thought of their brilliant little grins, their innocence and their exuberance. A lot of the time, when kids say this sort of stuff their parents go off their nut. The adults get so embarrassed, but they shouldn't; I'm blessed to be in that situation.

Kids make me feel special. Their innocence is heart-warming and reassuring. I'm sure all people are intrinsically good, until the world gets hold of them and makes some of them crooked and selfish. My favourite TV show, which I watch religiously (to the point that if I'm not home to watch it then I get it taped), is *Kids Say the Darndest Things*, which is hosted by the great Bill Cosby, who I think is absolutely fantastic.

Just as it is on this show, whenever you're around children, you never know what they're going to say, or how they're going to react. But you know they're going to mean it.

In contrast, I don't like some of the things I've said about people during my adult life, and some of the things that I've done, or the way I've done them. Some high-flyers might call that business, but I call it things I should have done differently. But I'd like to think that I've learnt from my mistakes and that I'll continue to learn from my mistakes. And I'd also like to think that I could, every now and then, rediscover the child in my heart. Not all the time, not even most of the time but *some* of the time. Once in a while we need to have fun, really enjoy that fun, and laugh like we've never laughed before.

You know what it's like to laugh until your face hurts. You get cramps in your cheeks, you want to stop laughing, but instead you laugh and laugh, more and more and more. Then your side starts hurting, your stomach starts cramping up. Kids know how to do that all the time. But then, they can do anything. If you're a parent, never tell your kids that they can't do something, because they can. Don't ask why, say, 'Hey, yeah. Why not?' Help them discover things, teach them to be themselves for the rest of their lives. Being you and no one else but you is all that matters.

Kimberley and Amanda, my brother Adam's two beautiful daughters, are very, very smart. They worked out long ago that because I need to walk on my hands, if they cross the road with me, they can't have their hands held, but for safety's sake they have to hold something. So they grab my ears. Which can pose a problem if Kimberley wants to go one way and Amanda wants to go the other.

One day, Kimberley came in to me while I was sitting on a lounge reading the newspaper and watching the TV. 'Uncle Half,' she said quietly, 'can I have a word to you for a minute?'

'Sure sweetheart,' I replied. 'What's the matter?'

Kimberley picked up the remote control and flicked off the TV. Then she took the paper off me and carefully folded it up before putting it down. This was important. She looked at me, that beautiful little face of hers so serious, and asked, 'Uncle Half, what do you want to be when you grow up?'

What do I want to be when I grow up! I was not too long past my thirtieth birthday, and felt that I'd already done plenty of growing up. What was my little goddaughter (I'm a godfather to both girls) trying to tell me? I wasn't sure what to say, or what Kimberley might have been expecting me to say. Initially I thought about shrugging my shoulders and putting the question in the proverbial 'too-hard basket'.

But then I looked at her again. 'Kimberley, darlin',' I said, 'I want to be a little kid for the rest of my life. I want to be able to have fun and enjoy myself whenever I want to. I want to be able to do the things that I want to be able to do. I really want to love life.'

Then I asked her, 'What do *you* want to be when you grow up?'

'I want to be just like you.'

And, you know, that made this stubborn, arrogant, pig-gish, stupid, snobbish man get up, walk away and have a little cry. What could I say to that? Absolutely nothing.

It made me feel so special.

The Gift of the Gab

ONE DAY I DID a speaking engagement in the city of Newcastle in New South Wales – it was a luncheon for the local 'corporates'. The presentation went well and at the end, as I usually do, I invited comments, feedback or questions from the audience. I was asked a range of questions but there was one that just blew me away.

The last thing I expected was for a 70-plus year old, white-haired man to stand up, with the help of his cane, and in a slow, gravelly voice come out with the question, loud across the auditorium, 'So, Mr Coutis, how's your sex life?'

The response from the audience was a mixture of smirks, chuckles and deafening silence. I had absolutely no idea what was the right thing to say, but before I could even gather my thoughts, from off-stage I heard my partner Trish shout back, '*Bloody fantastic!*' I think the old fella said 'Thank you very much' and then we all erupted into laughter. Well, all except me; I was just bright red with embarrassment. Trish's timing – and answer – could not have been better.

> **Evelyn Coutis:** Some people have the gift of the gab and some people don't. John's got it.

My very first *paid* speaking engagement, a few years before that unforgettable day, was for Steve 'Stumper' Rixon, the former New South Wales and Australian wicket-keeper, now New South Wales coach, and a long-time entrepreneur and sporting function organiser. This event was at the Concord RSL, for a Doug Walters luncheon put on by the NSW Cricket Association. Stumper gave me 15 minutes, that was it. The response was encouraging, and Stumper continued to use me from time to time. But way before that I used to go to church every Sunday morning with Dad and my Nan, to do the readings at the 7.30 service. That was my first experience talking in front of an audience.

> **Gary Coutis:** I wanted him to learn to read, and we used to get him up in church to do the readings. He said, 'I wouldn't mind doing that.' He used to sit in front of the pulpit and read, and that's where he first learnt to read and speak in front of people.

> He could read, he wasn't nervous. His Mum and I brought him
> up to be fearless, virtually fearless. Nothing was a problem once
> we got over the initial hurdles and the torment and bullying.

In truth I have an audience everywhere I go, whether it's shopping or to the beach, wherever. I feel as if I'm on display. So I've learnt to adapt and not be nervous in among or in front of people. People say that unless you're nervous you're not human, but while I might get a bit worked up about other silly things I never get nervous about speaking in public. In front of big crowds, the adrenalin might be pumping and I'll be raring to go, but I'm not nervous.

> **Steve Waugh:** It wasn't an earn for him, but he actually debuted
> with me around 1993, at a function out at Liverpool [in Sydney's
> south-western suburbs]. I got him up to say a few words and, of
> course, he stole the show. He did a couple of push-ups, and by
> the time he was finished everyone was talking about Johnno and
> had forgotten about me.
>
> Straightaway I knew there was a future there. He's always
> been a good talker and he's got a great story to tell. And he can
> motivate a lot of people.

In late 1996, James Knight, an outstanding reporter then working with the TEN network, did a story on me for the *Sports Tonight* show, which showed me playing indoor cricket, table tennis, weightlifting, all the things that most people didn't expect a bloke with my body to be able to do. As Brad Cooper – a high-profile motivational speaker and organiser of large-scale corporate functions – likes to tell people, he rolled over in bed, bumped the remote control, the TV came on and there I was. Brad's response, he continues, was to think, I can do something for this kid.

At this point in my life, I was working with the NSW Cricket Association as a development officer, and had been for a couple of years. I was going around to schools, coaching cricket, teaching the value of good hand–eye coordination skills, and was enjoying the role immensely. That position had evolved out of some of the cricket people I had met through Stephen, being associated with the Bankstown club. The Association was also finding that there were some disabled cricketers at the schools they were sending their development officers to. From there I found myself working with able-bodied cricketers as well and was put on the NSWCA payroll. And that's how I came into contact with James.

After Brad Cooper saw James's report on *Sports Tonight*, he contacted Alan Campbell at the NSWCA to set up a meeting. The opportunity he offered was fantastic – Brad set me on my way, there's no doubt about it.

I can remember my reaction when Brad first said, 'Johnno, I want you to get up on stage and speak.' It was something I had always wanted to do (well, to be honest, when I was younger I really wanted to be a stand-up comic, a sort of second coming of one of my heroes, Bill Cosby). And I had a good idea of what I wanted to say. For all Brad knew, I could have been going up there to give some race tips, but fortunately he had faith in me. I think, too, that he was curious to see what impact my physical appearance would have on the people in the audience. My message was straight to the point, the same mantra I will never step away from – if I can, you can. It went over a treat, and my career as a public speaker had begun.

It was as simple as 'get up there and have a go'. That first gig, all 300 seconds of it, went all right, as did the second one, and the one after that. I learnt a lot, kept badgering the professionals for advice about how to do things better, and went from there. Now, four years on, I've come a long way and I have got an awful long way to go. But I'll get there.

I've had the privilege of working on the speakers' circuit with many people who've helped and encouraged me, such as Lisa Curry-Kenny and her husband, Grant; Tom O'Toole, owner of Beechworth Bakery, one of Australian business's biggest success stories; Australia's No. 1 motivator, Mr Laurie Lawrence, whose talk will put goosebumps on your goosebumps; and ultra-marathon runner Pat Farmer. It turns out that Pat grew up in Granville, not far from where I live now, and as well as being a top bloke, he's almost as big a larrikin as I am. Another man who's taught me plenty is the former Grand Slam-winning Wallaby, now top-rating broadcaster, Alan Jones.

Alan Jones: There was an international symposium here and they had all these heavyweight speakers. I think Stormin' Norman from the Gulf War was there. I was one of two Australians asked to speak. It was quite peculiar, because I thought these were people who were supposed to be speakers but they had all these prepared texts and read them – which I don't think is essentially public speaking.

A friend of mine, Brad Cooper, brought John out at the end of it and he was an absolute hoot. And he was competent and he could speak. He's very funny, talking about himself, 'I just lobbed around the stage like a garden gnome.' He was a very articulate garden gnome.

I've never been formally trained in the art of public speaking and I never will. In my view, if you can't talk from the heart, you've got no right to be talking at all. Everything I say on stage is true. It's happened to me, it's how I think, it's what I believe is best.

Today I do the public speaking for the sheer enjoyment of it. If I can change one person's life when I'm on stage . . . that's why I do it. A million dollars can't buy that, neither can ten dollars. It's the pleasure. It's like when you're coaching someone in football or teaching someone at school and you see them practise it, learn it and do it the way that you taught them and it works.

A John Coutis presentation can be quite an emotional experience – for me and, hopefully, the audience. I combine humour with reality checks and ask people how they can put the things I talk about into their working and personal lives. My aim is to inspire individuals and work teams by my ability to take an active role in my own life and within the community. I want the individual or the corporation to turn their desire into action and results.

I am a very 'in your face' presenter. I do it a little differently from most, but that's just me. And the feedback I get from my presentations is that I can induce a major change in attitude and the way people view their lives and careers. I make people realise that their situations aren't that bad, that they can get out there and do whatever they want. I feel great when I hear that. It gives me a real sense of achievement.

After my talks I get letters and evaluation forms, and some of the things that come back to me are words and phrases such as 'I'm now willing to', 'I have a can-do attitude now', 'I'm prepared to go that extra step', 'Near enough is not good enough'. I love this kind of feedback.

I know that I'm certainly not everyone's cup of tea. Some people say I'm too loud, that I'm arrogant, that I'm too opinionated. I'm trying to learn from this, without losing who I am and what my message is. Sometimes, when someone has criticised my presentation as being 'a bit much', I think they just don't appreciate what I'm trying to do. Then I think, Well, you can't please everyone. In the end, it's up to the individuals to make a change, if that's what they want or need.

I always think, no matter what you are doing, that you should look to improve. From time to time I ask people I've worked with, who are also good friends, to sit in on my presentation to listen and offer feedback. This way I can make sure that what I am presenting is valuable, inspirational, and useful.

The youth of Australia is close to the hearts of both my wife Trish and me. I love my visits to schools and presenting to students. I focus on the ages 15 to 18 – years 10, 11 and 12. The school presentations are my way of giving something to the next generation, some ideas to carry with them through their lives and as they take up important roles within the community. The kids are fresh enough to be open to someone who is unusual, and are of a generation taught to celebrate things that are a bit different. They have not yet learnt to be afraid, to stare, touch or ask questions.

As much as I like presenting to adults (for adults, read people aged over 18), my biggest joy is interacting with kids, and professionally, my greatest satisfaction comes from talking to teenagers. I am astonished by the way kids aged between 12 and 18 will come up to me after I've spoken to a group of them and simply say, 'Thanks.' It's as if I'm the only one who can get through to them. But all I'm doing is telling my story, relating my hardships, explaining how I stayed positive and battled through. In doing so, I guess I don't belittle their own struggles; instead I give them something to compare themselves to. I give them hope, rather than preying on their fears. Hope builds, fear destroys.

I love watching the kids' reactions to what I say. I know that each and every one of them has a heart, and that my stories can reach that heart, and make them laugh, maybe once or twice make them cry. For one or two, I might make them cry out loud rather than keep their fears and insecurities locked up inside. Yet I look nothing like them, I'm twice their age, and the experiences on which I base my stories are really nothing special.

It doesn't matter who I'm speaking to, I speak the same way to adults as I do to teenagers. And the kids love that. I do talk about different things to the kids, but the manner in which I present myself is exactly the same. To me, I'm just being me and being honest.

I want the kids who listen to me to think, to be challenged, to be adaptable. My aim with the youth of Australia is to get them to dare to dream and learn to articulate those dreams, and to develop attitudes and habits aimed at success. I believe motivation comes from within. But inspiration, that comes from someone or something else, something outside. This is why I describe myself as an 'inspirational' speaker and not a 'motivational' one. My ambition is to inspire people, to influence them to motivate themselves and keep motivating themselves until they get where they want to go or become the person they want to be. I hope that the shock of seeing me and hearing me stays with them forever, that they remember that short, loud but inspirational fella they once listened to. I hope, too, that whoever has heard me picks up the message to get off their butts and go out there and make it happen, whatever it is they want to make happen; go for it and don't let anyone tell you that you can't do it.

There is nothing sweeter than doing something someone says you can't do!

It's a funny thing that humans follow their head instead of their heart. That to me is strange because without your heart your head doesn't work. I understand that there are many situations when you need to let the facts control your gut instincts, but often your heart is telling you to have a go, be brave, while your head wants you to play safe, don't get hurt, be ordinary. From my experience, there is nothing wrong with being brave. This said, there is plenty wrong with being stupid. I've learnt that, too.

The example I always use to illustrate the value of following your heart is the story of my first ride on a billycart. My head was telling me to go and sit on the lounge, while my pounding heart was screaming at me to get out there and have a go. 'But if you do go out there, you'll get hurt,' my brain was nagging. 'But think what you'll miss,' my heart replied. 'I don't want to embarrass myself.' 'Look at the fun Adam and Luke are having; you can do that.' 'What will Dad say?' 'Who cares, I can do it!' 'They'll laugh at me.' 'I'm gonna love it.' 'Maybe next time.' 'No, do it now!'

If my head had won that day, I honestly don't think I would have ever ridden that billycart. The next time, I'm sure my head would have won again. And think what I would have missed. That day, not only did I follow my heart, I became one of the boys.

It was the same when I got married. Geez, the first time I asked a girl out was a giant step, but getting married – wow! There were so many thoughts in my head, many of them quite logical, telling me not to get married, to play safe. Why risk everything? But I was in love, my heart kept reminding me, so marry Trish.

Do it now!

Love, Set, Match

BEFORE I INTRODUCE THE woman I share my life with, I just want to share a little information with you. I've already mentioned that the No. 1 question I get asked by kids is, 'Mr Coutis, how do you go to the toilet?' In fact a lot of parents wonder about that one, too, but the adults won't ask such questions. The answer? I go to the toilet the same way everybody else does. With teenagers, say from 14 to 19 years old, the most asked question is similar to that one the old bloke asked me in Newcastle, 'How do I have sex?' I never told that fella in the steel city because my partner (now wife), Trish, got in first. Now that I've had a couple of years to regain my composure, the answer I'd give him is, 'You don't need legs to have sex.'

I get all kinds of different questions put to me. All I ever try to do is answer them with honesty, a bit of humour, and with respect for the people who ask them. I'm grateful for their interest and their curiosity. All the things I talk about are true, and I'll always keep it that way.

I'm also often asked about Trish's response to my disability. Well, first I want to discuss my response to her disability. I manage to cope with her blonde hair.

Only joking!

I've already explained that moving out of home had been one of my biggest goals – to get my own place and show Mum and Dad that I was capable of looking after myself was something I desperately wanted to do. But when my first partner in this venture, my best friend Matthew, died just ten days after we opened the front door to our new life, it felt as if fate was saying, 'Johnno, I'm sorry but this independent thing is not for you.'

Despite everything I went through with Matthew's death, and everything else that had occurred in my life before that, I stayed put in that house. I'm still there today, living with my wife.

The first thing that hit me when I moved out was that there were a lot of things I had previously taken for granted that I now had to teach myself how to do. Let me tell you, if you live at home, you've most likely got it very, very easy. You probably have your parents taking care of you, maybe your Mum doing your washing and cooking and all sorts of very mundane but essential chores. I had to learn how to wash my own clothes, cook my own food, clean my own house. I had to work out how to use a vacuum cleaner, how to dust, just like a lot of other blokes have had to when they moved out. You realise it's not that hard, just different from what you're used to, and necessary. And these jobs come up more than once.

I also discovered that what is simple for most people can be disgracefully difficult for me. Putting a cup in a cupboard can be a challenge. Washing up – that can take hours.

If you've got legs, you walk into the kitchen, stand up, wash up. Easy. For me, it's no more difficult, just more time consuming. First I have got to get into my chair. Then I get up on my elbows to do the washing up. Drying up is worse and often costs me a plate or two. It's hard when one hand's holding the tea towel and the other is keeping your balance. Worst of all is the grill. It's bigger than me so what chance do I have? No wonder, when I'm home on my own, I often order Chinese and eat out of the container.

Another big challenge for me is making the bed. Stripping the bed is easy, but putting a sheet back on is terrible. I end up underneath the bloody thing, struggling to breathe. Half an hour later I feel as if I've been 15 rounds with Mike Tyson. Worst of all is trying to get the quilt back into the quilt cover. Inevitably I end up inside the thing.

I have a few special apparatuses in my house that help me do some of these things more easily. For example, in the kitchen I have one of those tall, hydraulic, office chairs on wheels, on which I can skate back and forth across the tiles. Nowadays I'm actually a bit of a whiz in the kitchen, which has become one of my favourite places. It's good because Trish and I can dance as well as cook when I'm on that chair, and you can always catch me in the kitchen, whipping from the oven to the sink to the hotplates to the microwave to the fridge. It's like bloody dodgem cars in there sometimes, the two of us bumping into each other, but it's still all good fun.

Trish got a bit of a culture shock when she first came to visit my humble abode because the place is fitted out for people in wheelchairs. There are ramps into and out of the house, the door handles are down low, the light switches are down lower still, and there are no cupboards under the kitchen benches. Poor Trish, who's six foot two, has to bend her back to do something as complicated as putting a bit of light on the subject.

But I'm getting ahead of myself. The story of our relationship began in early 1997, when I was in Perth for a Winning Edge seminar, with Brad Cooper and two high-flying corporate types, Siimon Reynolds and Bob Pritchard. There were two seminars scheduled for the Western Australian capital, but I was only involved in the first of them because I needed to get back to Sydney, where I was due to compete in the Multi-Disability Games.

After my presentation in Perth, I was surrounded by hundreds of people who wanted to say g'day, get an autograph or have their photograph taken with me. This was still all new to me, and while I loved it I did find it pretty intense and very tiring. In the middle of it, something made me look up – I don't know what it was, but today I'm so thankful that I had this feeling. I looked up to see this beautiful, elegant, stunning young lady walk across the back of the auditorium, towards the foyer. But she wasn't looking at me, only at where she was going. Which was out. I'm saying to myself, 'Why aren't you in this line, coming to say g'day? Please come and say hello, I'd love to meet you.'

Unfortunately that didn't happen. I kept one eye on her as she moved closer to the exit, and one on the people right in front of me. She's getting closer and closer and closer to the door; my chance of meeting her is going. 'Please stop, come and say hello, that's all I want. Please, I just want to know your name.' Eventually she reaches that door and then she – stops. She stops and turns around. Can you believe it? And now she's walking back, back towards me!

She joins the queue. So now I'm ploughing through the autographs. Whereas before I was chatting and laughing and writing short, inspiring messages with my signature, now it's just, 'G'day, where do you want me to sign? Okay.' (Sign simply 'John Coutis'.) 'Nice to meet you. Next!'

Finally she's standing right in front of me.

'G'day, John,' she began assuredly. 'I'm Trish van Leeuwen, President of WA Disabled Sports, and I just wanted to come over and say hello. We're sending our team over to New South Wales for the Nationals, I think they're on the same flight as you are this afternoon. You know, I shouldn't be saying this to you, being from a different state, but good luck.'

She'd taken an interest in me. That's what I was thinking. In *me*, rather than just in my message. Everyone else in that line had come up to say g'day and express thanks for what I had done for them. But I could see in those lovely ocean blue eyes of hers that she had an interest in how I was going. A small difference – and please don't think that I'm having a go at anyone else who was in that queue – but for me it was a very important and significant difference. As I flew back to Sydney, I wasn't thinking about anyone else who'd been in that auditorium.

Only Trish van Leeuwen.

Of WA Disabled Sports.

That's all I knew, but it was a start.

A couple of months later I was speaking at a High Achievers weekend in Brisbane, which was again organised by Brad Cooper. And Trish was there; I recognised her straightaway. On the final night, I went up to her and said, 'G'day.' We started talking about sport and cracking a few jokes, and gradually worked our way out of the crowd to a much quieter spot in a hallway outside the room.

One thing I immediately loved about Trish was that she sat on the ground to talk to me. She didn't stand up and stare down at me, she sat on the ground and took an interest. Trish had a red wine in her hand; I wasn't drinking.

Two guys who had clearly had a couple of quiet drinks together suddenly staggered down the corridor. They were lucky the hallway had walls because that meant they walked in a reasonably straight line.

'Oh, John, howyagoin'?' one of them tried to say.

'G'day boys, how are you?' I replied, and before they responded (I could tell how they were) I added, 'Have you met my fiancée, Trish?'

Before this night, I'd met this woman once. The two blokes looked at me, at Trish, then each other. Even if they'd been sober, I doubt they would have said anything. Then Trish said, 'Look, I'm sorry guys, we'd love to chat, but this is the only time I've got with him and I'm actually trying to set a wedding date.'

They were out of there quick smart, while Trish and I just looked at each other and laughed and laughed. I was having such a good time. But I wasn't thinking of Trish as a potential girlfriend, or anything like. She's way out of my league, I thought at the time. Still do. When I was growing up, disabled people didn't get married. Or if they did, their partner was also disabled.

Trish was clearly highly intelligent. She is very good looking. I'm a boofhead. She's tall, and she's able-bodied. There were five good reasons why I wasn't thinking of her as a future partner. We were just having fun.

Eventually my 'minders' came and found me, to take me back to my room. About 30 metres down the hallway, I turned and yelled out, 'Honey, I'll see you back in the room.' And Trish burst out laughing again.

Later I found myself again in Perth, and I'm at the stage where I really like this lady, in fact I adore her, and I said to myself, 'Johnno, go for broke. You don't know, she's only going to say no.' Rejection is a part of life. But no one had told me that Trish was also General Manager of WA Netball. I made about 200 calls trying to track her down. Finally I located her, and she agreed to come out for dinner. I suggested a foursome, one of her friends and my mate and minder Joe Hutton making up the quartet. You beauty.

I booked a table at the Sicilian in Subiaco, because the Sicilian Restaurant back in Parramatta had always taken good care of me. Sure enough, when we got there they'd picked out bottles of wine for us, which was brilliant except for the fact that because of my physical make-up alcohol affects my body much more quickly than it does bigger people. By the time the desserts had been eaten, we were loud and boisterous, me especially so, and then in the carpark at the Subiaco Hotel afterwards I put on a bit of a show, climbing up a 'No Standing' sign to wave a loud and heartfelt goodbye, and all in all put one big exclamation point on what had been one of the best nights of my life.

I'll never forget one joke we played that evening. At the pub after dinner, we were sitting on a lounge. I was right up one end, with my back resting on the arm of the lounge. Trish was sitting up straight, right next to me, at a 90-degree angle to how I was sitting. If you didn't know us and you looked at us, it would have seemed as if she was sitting on my lower lap and upper legs, with her friend Sharon, next to her, sitting on my lower legs.

A waitress came up and I complained to her that this

girl was sitting on me and wouldn't get off. It was the old joke I'd played before, though Trish had never been a part of it before. But she played her part perfectly.

'C'mon, darl,' I said in front of this waitress. 'Please get off so I can move.'

Trish said, 'No, no.'

'Well, can you just grab my arm and pull me out?' I asked the waitress.

Which she did. And, of course, my body spat out immediately and the waitress almost died. When she calmed down she laughed, too (as people always do when I play out this prank), though she did threaten to send me a bill for counselling.

Trish van Leeuwen: I first met John at a conference at the Burswood Casino in Perth. I was there as the General Manager of WA Netball and John was a surprise guest. All I can remember from his presentation is laughing until I cried; I could picture the stories he was telling and the reaction from people around him. I can remember thinking of him, What a great example of living life to the max and having a great attitude and a sense of humour to go with it. I love it when someone can make me laugh.

I was walking out of the auditorium when I recalled that John had mentioned he was flying back to Sydney for the Multi-Disability Games. At the time I was also the President of the Western Australian Disabled Sports Association and knew we had a team going to these Games. Before I left, I thought I'd quickly go and wish John good luck.

There were a lot of people milling around John, so I stood

back and watched him 'in action'. He had a big smile on his face, as person after person told him he was 'great' and 'brilliant' and 'inspiring', that he was 'an amazing disabled person'. Gradually, ever gradually, his smile turned from being fuelled by adrenalin to one that might have been a little forced. When it was my turn I put my hand out and introduced myself. He smiled at me, with a relieved look on his face that said, 'Thank God you're someone who knows what it's all about.'

I remember his face just lifting and lighting up.

It was a very brief conversation, maybe all of a minute, and I ended with, 'Good luck, hope you do well. Look out for the team from West Oz and go up and say hi.' All this was pretty quick.

That conference had a follow-up program on the Gold Coast a couple of months later. It was an intensive three days, and once again John was one of the guest speakers. When the conference was finally completed, I was in the foyer with about 450 other people who were exhausted from all the full-on work. All of a sudden, this 'thing' wrapped itself around my leg and scared the living daylights out of me. I jumped through the roof. Then I looked down and there was John, who had picked me out of a crowd of 900 legs.

I said, 'Oh, hi.' Immediately, I sat down on the floor so I was at eye level – as you do – and we started to chat. With 450 people around we were quickly trodden on and I had an immediate glimpse into John's world of people not seeing you and standing on your fingers. We just chatted about the Multi-Disability Games and sport for the disabled. We had lots in common because of our backgrounds, and I was amazed he remembered me from that 60-second conversation back in Perth.

A couple of months later, my assistant at WA Netball rang through to my office and said, 'Trish, I've got a John Coutis on the phone for you.'

I've picked up the phone and the first thing I hear is, 'You are the hardest lady in the world to find!'

When John invited me to join him and his friend for dinner I was a bit unsure at first, but knew it was something I had to do. I got on the phone to my best mate, Sharon, and said, 'You've got to come with me, I don't want to go by myself.' It was so 'girlie'.

After dinner, we went across to the Subiaco Hotel and had them all guessing. A lady who had heard John speak came up, and this time he introduced me as his wife! And Joe and Sharon as being engaged. All four of us just jumped into this role-play, Joe and Sharon taking on their roles without batting an eyelid. I could not believe how this night was evolving. It was different, entertaining and very funny. I was fascinated and amused by the people's reactions around us. We were laughing at the world – and at ourselves!

I saw John for coffee before he went back to Sydney; I sent a thank-you card to him for dinner; he called; we started to write. I then travelled to Canberra for the national netball championships, where we rendezvoused because he supposedly was training at the Australian Institute of Sport – I found out later he had rigged it and just wanted to catch up – and it all went from there.

I really enjoy our conversations. From the start, I loved his attitude and his humour, the way he laughs at the world and at himself. He knows he is different and he likes to either make people feel at ease around him by starting the conversation or just by saying hello. Other times, when he thinks someone or something isn't right or fair, he will make loud noises to challenge you or make you think a little bit more.

Before too long, I felt at home with John. Sharon expressed it best when she said to me, 'He challenges you physically, emotionally, spiritually and intellectually, and you are someone who needs all of that.'

By November 1997, we were just about in a serious relationship. 'Trish,' I asked her quietly one day, 'you don't see my disability, do you?'

I was sure she'd flatly and quickly say, 'No.' But instead she replied very honestly, looking me straight in the eye, 'Well, yes, I do.'

I was absolutely gobsmacked. I didn't know what to say. I just thought, Oh, geez, what have I got myself into?

Then she added, 'But they'll never find a cure for such a sick sense of humour, so I'll just have to put up with it.'

This is a woman who gives as good as she gets. This was the woman for me.

One of the toughest things I've done that involved my relationship with Trish occurred one day when we were together in Canberra, not long after we'd started dating. I took her into one of the big shopping centres in the nation's capital, and just did what I always do. Which was to buzz around on my skateboard, often holding her hand, giving her a hug, having a good time. Inevitably, everyone was looking at me, some sneaking a peek over their shoulder, some staring, some pointing, a few giggling. It was something that I had to do, for her sake, because it was going to make or break the relationship. They weren't sneaking a peek over their shoulder, or staring, or pointing, or giggling at me, they were doing so at us. You could sense the curiosity of many people watching us – 'What the hell is the matter with her?' 'What on earth is she doing with him?' 'What could she possibly see in him?'

I could tell that Trish wasn't enjoying the experience very much. At the food court, we ordered our meals and then sat in a little corner, and I said, 'Trish, darlin', how do you feel right now? I need to know.'

She admitted she didn't quite know how to cope. 'Welcome to my world,' I said.

'You know,' Trish mumbled, 'your world stinks.'

And I said simply, 'Maybe.' Then I added, 'Many people's perceptions of me and reactions to me are absolutely terrible. You do have your good ones, but you really need to make up your mind about which way you're going to go with this. If you don't want to be in this relationship, that's fine. If you think you can't handle it,' I said, 'that's fine, too, but I can't make that decision for you.'

I assumed the experience would have been the end of her, but it wasn't. A few years on and we're still together. I guess I was a real bastard to spring that on her, but I knew what I was doing.

Trish van Leeuwen: Often at John's presentations it seems as if nearly as many people come up to me as they do to John. In John's case, the mix is pretty much 50:50, men and women.

John usually has a real impact on women. Personally, though, I always find it interesting to watch what the men do and what they ask, because I know that men can be just as sensitive as women, even if they are usually reluctant to express their feelings. If they are showing their emotions, then I know that John has cut at the core of their psyche.

One of the most asked questions of me is how did we meet? That is usually followed by how do we cope? Translated, this means how do we cope with our physical differences? All the while, the people's body language is suggesting there are a few more tricky questions bottled up inside. The physical aspect of our relationship is always a subject of intrigue. It's usually unspoken, but their eyes are ultra-curious. They might try to word the question in another way. 'How do you guys get on?' they might ask with a knowing look, a nod of the head or a sly wink.

I don't intend to go into the ins and outs of our sex life, except to say that I have a great sex life, thank you very much.

But even this is not the most nagging of those bottled-up questions. For many, when they talk to me, or just see me, the query is simple: 'Why John?'

Why would an able-bodied woman choose to be in a relationship with a physically disabled man such as John?

It's not something I can answer easily, yet really it is a simple, wonderful tale of two people with a lot in common falling in love. Whenever I tell the story about how we met, almost everyone responds, 'What a great story, what a great way to meet!' Why? I think it's because this uncomplicated yarn perfectly captures John's very quick wit, his larrikinism, his sense of humour. And it also shows that I give as good as I get, that we are well matched.

I guess if you're going to start a relationship, any relationship, you've got to have some common ground. John likes to crack sharp, quick-witted remarks, and I like people who have a snappy wit about them. I enjoy being with people who can make me laugh, people who entertain me. John can certainly do that. With him, I also loved the fact that amid our wisecracks, we'd rapidly get into a role-play – a kind of street theatre if you like – as if we're in our own little drama.

I was working with people with disabilities long before I met John. The standard that underpins my approach to my career and life is that everyone deserves a 'quality of life'. No one, in my view, has a right to stop another from having a quality life. It's not a compassion thing, it's not a sympathy thing; only very, very rarely will someone with a disability get my sympathy. My question to them will be, 'Do you want a quality life and, if you do, what do we have to do for you to get it?'

Because I have worked for so long with people with disabilities, when a disabled person crosses my path I just don't see the disability. Of course, I see the wheelchairs, the absence of legs, or arms, or whatever. But I don't react to that disability and I haven't for many years. My response is that there is a person, and if I think they are interesting or I can help them achieve a quality life – in other words, if there is a chance for us to have a mutually rewarding association – then I would like to get to know that person.

When I couldn't understand why people were shocked, unsure or questioning of my relationship with John, my best friend Sharon came to the rescue again with one simple statement that put it all in perspective. 'John is an extension of your normal life.' I had spent so much time around children and people with either learning difficulties or disabilities; it wasn't until I saw the scepticism about our relationship that I realised that there are a great many more people who haven't mixed with disabled people. Only to them is this not normal.

This conundrum was everywhere around me, but it took my relationship with John to bring it to the surface. One of the most vivid memories I have is when I told my parents I was serious about John. My Mum sat me down at the kitchen table and asked, 'Trish, when are you going to do something normal?' I looked back at her and said, 'I hope I never do, Mum.' She just couldn't quite comprehend it. Then she and Dad sat me down and said, 'We love you, and we think you are choosing a very hard road. We are worried about you. Are you sure this is what you want? Are you sure you are aware of the consequences? Do you get what you are doing? And, Trish, are you really, really sure?'

All I could do was keep reminding myself that my Mum and Dad were coming from a position of love and, as parents, were simply trying to protect their child. In reply, I kept telling them that I have never lived my life any other way than doing what I want to do.

I love being around people who say, 'Yes we can do that, we can have a go at that. I like your goals, I like your dreams, and good luck, I'm right behind you all the way.' John is someone who doesn't laugh or ridicule my goals and my dreams.

Of course, this is far from a normal physical relationship. After all, I'm two foot six and my wife is six foot two. So why did Trish stay? Because, I reckon, she is a very tough nut, often opinionated but also warm, loyal, caring, affectionate, romantic, loving, and she believes in herself. Fortunately, she loves me, and just as fortunately, she is strong enough to see beyond the physical imbalance and recognise that such a romance can work.

And anyway, what is normal these days? 'Normal' is a funny word. I do what I can around the house and Trish does what she can around the house. I have my independence and she has her independence. For a while before we met, I was about doing absolutely everything for myself – shopping, washing, lawns, vacuuming, household chores. Now I have a partner in my life who shares these jobs. Trish is the same. We, as a couple, are like all other couples in this regard.

When I was single and had to go to the supermarket, I used to carry the plastic bags full of groceries in my mouth from the checkout to the boot of my car. This meant two things: one, I used to go to the supermarket a lot because I could only buy so much at a time, and, two, my jaws were the best-exercised part of my body. Now I don't need to do this, because I've got someone to push a trolley. I have to admit that my life is now much easier. The down side is that I've got a bit lazier – no, a lot lazier – which is something I'm trying to change.

With or without Trish, shopping is an expedition not to be missed. With her, it can be so much fun, though maybe not for those around us. The supermarket is a stage where 'almost anything goes'. Every now and again, I get Trish to put me in the trolley. You'll have to imagine this one – the trolley is getting fuller and the food and stuff is piling up around me, to the point that all that is poking out among the groceries is my head.

One time, we were into our last aisle, and Trish stopped to go back and grab something she'd forgotten. Meanwhile, a woman leant across our trolley to get something off the shelf directly above me. As she leant over, I said nonchalantly, 'Would you pass me one of those too, please?'

This poor woman must have jumped about three metres, knocking groceries everywhere as she flew. A talking grocery trolley!

Eventually we ended up at the checkout, where Trish calmly unpacked the trolley while I sat as still as I could. All the while, the checkout chick was looking at me, as more and more of my body was revealed. Finally, I was all that was left, and with the poor girl at the cash register totally confused, Trish looked at her with a straight face and said, 'You'll need to call for a price check. I couldn't find a price tag anywhere on him, I don't know how much he costs.'

Trish van Leeuwen: There are two things I miss most because of John's disability. The first is someone to take out the rubbish bin, help me bring in the shopping from the car, to carry the suitcases. The second is cheek-to-cheek, slow dancing. I don't think there is anything more romantic or seductive than being able to hold somebody while in the background there is slow music.

But John and I are working on that. He has a hydraulic chair in the kitchen, which we make as tall as we can and then we Ginger-Rogers-and-Fred-Astaire around the place. He's still learning the steps, because he's afraid of heights and doesn't like being spun around. But we'll get there.

Other than those two things, I have a regular guy and a regular life that has some extraordinary experiences in it. We live the same up-and-downs as everybody else.

One day in Perth, towards the end of 1997, Trish came home from work and was busy in the kitchen. I walked in and I don't know how, but the topic of marriage came up.

Straightaway she looked at me and said, 'I want to get engaged, I want to get married.'

My first thought was, Bloody hell!

What was I supposed to think?

Getting married to the woman I loved had been a dream of mine. I couldn't believe that it was going to come true. I asked Trish to come into the lounge room, where we sat down on the floor and started having a bit of a chat. Then I stopped her in mid-sentence and said, 'Trish, I want to make a deal with you.'

'Okay,' she said.

'If you can find a groom doll for the wedding cake without any legs,' I continued, 'then I'll marry you.'

'That's no problem,' said Trish. 'I've already got that worked out. I'm just going to push him further into the cake.'

To be frank, I wasn't overly happy with that detail.

In mid February Trish was visiting from Western

Australia, and we decided to go into the city to spend some time in the shops. I told Trish that we couldn't stay out too late because I wanted to take her out to dinner. Unbeknown to her I had organised a very special evening.

I drove us into town and stopped outside the Hyatt on the Harbour, had the car valet parked, and took Trish into the foyer. Trish sat near the grand piano and I hopped up and fiddled with the keys. 'What are we doing here?' she asked, and I replied that I'd organised for a car to drive us about the city. A bit of a sightseeing adventure. Something different.

'A car?'

'Yeah, a car.'

A limo pulled up. 'Nuh, that's not it,' I said. Then another. 'Nuh, not that one either.' Then a third one, this time a stretch limo. And then a horse and carriage.

'Mr Coutis?' asked the driver.

'That's right.'

'Mr Coutis, your chariot awaits.'

Trish could not believe it! The woman's sense of theatre was magnificent.

We rode slowly around The Rocks area of Sydney, sipping on a fashionable bottle of red, until we pulled up in a quiet spot in the park on Observatory Hill, underneath the Bridge, overlooking the Harbour. I pulled the ring out of my pocket and asked my lover to marry me, formalising that conversation we'd had in the kitchen back in Perth. I cannot tell you how wonderful this moment was. For the next hour, we were on the phone telling everybody we were engaged.

Telling everyone just how happy we were.

Face to Face
with Cancer

THE FIRST INKLING I got that something was seriously wrong with my health came in the second half of 1999. I was on a speaking tour, and for no reason at all, not for nerves, I'd have to run to the toilet to vomit. Then I'd be really, really tired. And I'd burst out in sweats. But I didn't worry about it too much because I thought it was just caused by the workload, by doing too much. This was Mother Nature saying, 'Johnno, you've just got to slow down a little.'

But my sleeping patterns were awful, too. I'd be out like a light, then wide awake. This had been going on since the beginning of the year, I reckon, but I lived with it because I was loving what I was doing. I was an in-demand public speaker, I was engaged to be married. Then one day I found myself out in country New South Wales, having done a speaking gig at a school at Condobolin, and being driven to Parkes airport. I kept thinking back to that talk, and how I'd felt pretty uncomfortable around the groin, and how it bit a little when I went to the toilet. However, I was raised with the attitude that if it's not bleeding, it's not hurting, and I know – I guess because of what I've had to grow up with – that I have a stronger pain tolerance than most. But that road from Condobolin to Parkes seemed pretty bloody bumpy.

For much of the flight I was kind of green around the gills, as they say. By the time I was in the cab going home, I was worried. And after I finally made it through the front door and staggered straight to the bathroom, I couldn't help but notice how swollen my left testicle was. It was sore to touch; in fact I was sore all around the groin area. I took a couple of Panadol, lay down on my bed, and hoped that it would go away.

Come midnight, maybe 12.30, I knew I had to go to hospital. I couldn't touch my left testicle now, but instead of calling an ambulance, as I should have, I rang a cab. Consequently, when I arrived at Casualty they had no idea how crook I was, and I had to take a seat and wait my turn. I was in a lot of pain; most people, I figure, would have been tearing down walls.

After around 45 minutes a nurse came out, and I yelled

out at her, 'Please help me, I'm in pain.' She registered me and asked what the problem was. I told her, and she said, 'Okay, the doctor will be here to see you soon.'

'Thank you,' I said. 'You beauty.'

For the next several hours I sat with a couple of others in the waiting room. Ambulances brought in one or two emergency cases, and a woman was rushed in after giving birth to her baby in the back of a car. I was thinking, 'I'll just wait my turn and not say too much, just put up with it.'

But by six o'clock I couldn't cope any longer. Still, no one had come out to see me. I hadn't moved, hadn't been game to move an inch in case I'd lost my spot. Finally, I staggered up to the nurse and yelled, 'I need to see a doctor *now*.'

She said, 'Please settle down.'

But I was past that. 'I've been here for five-and-a-half hours,' I roared. 'I told you when I came in here that I had a pain in my groin. You've got no idea what it's like now. You don't know what it's like. Please get me a bloody doctor.'

Soon after, I was in to see a doctor. He took one look at my testicle and said, 'My God, how long have you been sitting there like this?'

'Since 12 bloody 30!'

He gave me some painkillers, thank God. Then he had a closer look and a poke and a prod and said, 'I think it's a UTI, a urinary tract infection; that's why it's all swollen.'

And I replied, 'I was hoping that's what you'd say,

because I'm going to Brisbane in a few hours. I've got to go home and pack and make my way to the airport.'

'What are you doing up there?' he asked.

'I'm going up with the Australian cricket team to watch the guys play.'

This was early November 1999. We had a very brief chat about the sport, the team, and how I'd got involved. 'I'll put you on a course of antibiotics,' he told me, which I thought meant he was going to give me some pills, but instead they stuck an IV in me and ran the antibiotics straight through my system. I was happy because the pain had gone away, but whether that was because of the painkillers or the antibiotics I didn't know. I did notice as I prepared to make my way to the airport that the swelling hadn't gone away.

By the time I reached the departure lounge, my groin region was niggly, but nothing like it had been. I was travelling with a very good friend of mind, John Baxter, or 'Alvin' as we all know him, and he took one look at me and said, 'Geez, you look terrible.'

I said, 'Mate, I've just come from the bloody hospital.'

'Oh, shit. Are you going to be all right to fly?'

'Yeah, I'll be all right. The doc gave me some painkillers and told me what to do to look after myself. I'm pretty sure I'll be okay.'

In truth, I probably wasn't okay, but thanks to the beautiful staff at Qantas, who on this occasion gave us an upgrade to business class, I got there. Through the flight I drank heaps of water, even though urinating was difficult, every bump was a mile high, and when we landed I went straight from my hotel room to the hospital.

For some reason I hadn't had an ultrasound in Sydney, but the doctors in Brisbane thought I needed one now. It took around 45 minutes for an ultrasound machine to become available, and in that time I rang Trish to tell her where I was. 'It's never dull with you, is it?' was her immediate response. Then she asked, 'What do you think is wrong with you?'

I honestly didn't know. I thought perhaps I had a twisted testicle, and that they'd operate, untwist it and everything would be okay. I mean, it couldn't be any worse than that or the doc in Sydney would have said so.

The young doctor at the hospital was terrific. As soon as he had the ultrasound result, and after it had been studied by a gaggle of specialists, he looked me straight in the eye and said, 'John, this has to come out now.'

The testicle itself was twisted, and blood circulation around it and in it had stopped. The testicle was dead. I kept thinking, when is this pain going to stop?

'When did you start getting sore?' the doc asked.

'Yesterday, lunchtime.'

'Why didn't you go to a hospital in Sydney?'

'I did.'

'What did they say?'

'They said it was probably a urinary tract infection.'

'John,' the doc said sternly, 'you've got to have that testicle removed now.' They put me into a ward, and while I waited for the surgeon, I rang Trish, my parents, Alvin,

Steve Waugh and some cousins in Brisbane. 'If you've got time,' I said to the rels, 'come and say g'day.'

So there I was in the hospital, and as I knew what was wrong, I was feeling okay. I was relaxed, a little apprehensive but no more so than anyone else who's ever faced surgery. The first day of the cricket Test was on the TV, so I couldn't have been happier, except for where I was. The doctor came in and went through a detailed explanation of the procedure, but halfway through I cut him off and said, 'Mate, can you do me a favour? Can you ring my Mum and tell her? She's a nurse and will be able to explain it to me in language I understand.' So the doc – gee, he was a good bloke – got straight on the phone to Mum, and then Mum called me and told me I was going to be fine. Around 7 pm, I went into surgery and all I could think of was that the pain was going to be gone. Boom, under the knife I go.

When I came to, I was in the recovery ward, in with some other patients, plus nurses, nuns and doctors. Through the blur from the after-effects of the anaesthetic I saw my doctor approaching, and yelled out at the top of my voice, 'Here he comes, the testicle fairy!' Everyone laughed. It wasn't the sort of thing they heard in that room too often. The good news was the doc was happy, and a few hours later I was wheeled back to my room, where Stephen and Alvin were waiting for me. Unfortunately, I wasn't really up for conversation. I crashed out and didn't wake until well into the second day of the Test.

When the doctor saw me after I woke, he told me that

I needed to stay in hospital for a month. I said, 'I beg your pardon.'

'You need to be here for a month,' he repeated, 'because of the way you sit – the fact you sit on your groin – and what you do and how you get around. I'm sorry, mate. You need that time for it to recover properly.'

'Doc, I'm sorry,' I said. 'I can't do that. I'm up here to go to the cricket, you know. I'll stay in another couple of nights, fine, but I've got work to do next week. I've got speaking engagements in Sydney. I've got kids relying on me and people relying on me. I'm committed to them. I'm not staying in here a month, there's no way in the world I can do that.'

If the doc hadn't already figured out I was a difficult patient, he knew it now.

'John, the testicle you've lost, we could have used it as a cricket ball. The one that's left, it doesn't look perfect either, you've got to be careful.'

I wasn't really listening. I wanted out of there. He also told me that they'd sent the removed testicle for a biopsy, but that was standard procedure. Then I got up to go to the toilet, and I couldn't move. It hurt to move. Oh, shit. Maybe I will be in here for a month. But things did start to get better very quickly, to the point where I signed myself out during the late afternoon and returned to my hotel.

The doctor was a little bit angry, but you've got to do what you've got to do. I'd admitted myself into hospital, I could sign myself out. I went back to the hotel, went out for dinner that night and then on the Sunday I went down to the cricket. That day, while I was sitting in front of the Australian dressing room, I got my melon on the television coverage, which did nothing for my Mum's peace of mind when she saw it. I stayed for a little while, but I was kidding myself. The ache got worse and worse, and before the day was through I'd called Qantas, changed my flight, and was on my way home.

As soon as I could on the Monday, I saw my doctor and told him what had happened. When he checked me out he told me I'd been silly to leave hospital so quickly, but that everything was fine. On the Tuesday morning, though, I got a call to say that they wanted to do some more blood tests. And after those tests came another call, asking me to go and see a specialist.

No matter what they do to dress them up or how often you've been there, doctors' surgeries are still sterile, spiritless places. You never quite feel comfortable in one. No room for fun. On this day, a Tuesday in November 1999, I was in a room I had never been in before, face to face with a specialist I'd never met before. It was just a couple of days after the operation in Brisbane to remove my left testicle. I didn't know why I was in that specialist's rooms. I did know I was well on the way to recovering from the recent surgery. I was getting better. Or so I thought.

'John,' this doctor said without a shred of emotion, 'I've got your results and it looks as though you've got testicular cancer.'

Just like that.

'What!' I said, totally aghast. 'What do you mean? Where did that come from?'

Where *did* that come from?

'You have testicular cancer,' he said again. He then continued, 'There are two types; if they catch it quickly –'

'I've got *cancer*?'

'If they catch it pretty quickly, they can fix it. If they can't –'

'Well,' I butted in, 'thank God they took it out.'

'Ah, well, I'm afraid the other one's got to go, too.'

Can we slow down for a minute? To this point, even when I'd had that operation in Brisbane, it had never crossed my mind that I wouldn't be able to have kids. Losing my left ball had been a bit of a slight on my manhood, yes, but never had I thought about not being able to have a family. As I'd sat in the waiting room, I'd been thinking about how good I'd been feeling. Two minutes ago, I was recovering. Now, all that I could think about was – I want to have kids! Instead, this bloody quack was telling me there was no time to even think about saving my sperm.

'I'm sorry, John, we have to move quickly.'

The operation to remove my last testicle was simple and relatively painless. But in the aftermath of that surgery, as more results of more tests came in, a sense of urgency grew and grew. Soon I was being told that the cancer had spread, that the doctors didn't like what was happening.

Throughout, I kept the fact I had cancer completely to myself. I didn't tell Trish, I didn't tell my parents, or any of my friends. I mean, how could I? I had been fighting for my life for 30 bloody years, and now I had cancer. How did they want me to tell my Mum and Dad, who had been taking care of me for 30 years, sacrificing plenty for 30 years, that it had all been just to end like this? For cancer. I'd rather get hit by a bus – boom, my life's over – than have this.

And then came the king hit. The doctor, this bloke I hardly knew, said, 'John, our best estimation is you have 12 to 24 months left to live.'

'What are you telling me?'

'Twenty-four months,' the doctor said again. 'I'm sorry, but we don't think you'll get anything more than that.'

I was so angry. How dare this bloke tell me that. I climbed up on his desk and knocked everything off it onto the floor. 'Listen here,' I roared. 'Who the hell gives you the right to tell me when I'm going to die? Is it that stethoscope around your neck? The glasses on your head? Because you're a doctor?

'I'll die when I'm good and ready to die, not when somebody like you tells me I'm going to die.'

He was leaning back in his chair while I was on the very edge of his desk, three inches from his face. I'd been spitting on him as those angry words sprayed out. I didn't say anything else, just climbed back down off the desk, onto the chair and out the door. All I could think of was how was I going to tell my Mum and Dad? The doctor, God bless him, rushed out after me into the reception. He turned me around and gave me a really big hug. And he was crying, too. He wiped his eyes and he wiped mine, and then he said, 'That's what'll beat it.'

'What, me yelling like that?'

'No, that attitude, that mindset will beat this.'

Gavin Robertson: John got me to come down to this speaking function. There were heaps of people, about 4000 or 5000 people, there that night, and he was speaking to them and blowing them away. He got a standing ovation at the end.

He got off, and I said, 'How you going?'

He said, 'I want to go, I'm not feeling real good.'

So we get in the car and we're driving home, and he says to me, 'I've got testicular cancer.' Just hits me with it after that function.

Tom O'Toole: At first I thought the poor bugger was buggered. But, boy oh boy, his confidence and his positive attitude was absolutely mindboggling. Here he was, just out of hospital, getting up on stage and working. He would have to lay on his back to try and conserve his energy, he was that weak, but was still getting out there and doing a fantastic job, and being so happy and laughing.

I spoke to John many times when he was sick, and he always gave me a laugh. Always. And that is pretty bloody incredible.

I don't regret exploding in front of the doctor; that's the way I am. I did apologise to him, and he said, 'Don't worry, it was actually quite placid compared to what some people have said. I guess I wasn't expecting you to be so in my face.'

And I said, 'Well, mate, that's me, very much in your face.'

As I drove away from that meeting, having just been told that I had two years max to go, one thought kept going through my head: I'm going to die. I'm going to die.

I'm going to die.

This continued for most of the journey home. How am I going to tell Trish? I'm going to die. How do I tell Mum and Dad?

I'm going to bloody die.

But by the time I got home, I was calmer. Maybe I can beat it. How am I going to beat it? There were so many things I wanted to do. Suddenly, just like that, maybe I'd run out of time. I asked myself two questions: 'What is most important to me?' and 'Where is my time best spent?' I wasn't thinking about the next two years. I was thinking about now, today.

I had to search deep inside myself to discover how much strength I had. Frankly, I didn't think I was as strong as I turned out to be. I knew I was tough; I had to have been to cope with what I've put up with over the last 30 years, but this was something new. Scary. Shit, I was scared. I didn't know how those around me were going to handle it; I didn't know how I was going to handle it. I didn't know how I was going to tell those close to me, what I was going to say, or whether I'd be able to stay in one piece when I did. First up, I told Trish.

Of course, she was terribly upset. 'I'll pack my bags,' my fiancée said quickly, 'I'll be over tomorrow.'

But I said, 'Look, no. That's the last thing I want. I need some time, I need some time for me. I've got to get my head around this.'

We decided to spend a week apart – to sort ourselves out a bit – and then we'd come back together to deal with it as a couple.

Trish van Leeuwen: WA Netball and I had already come to an agreement where I would finish my contract early, and our plan had been that I would have some time before Christmas 1999 where I would pack up the house and have Christmas at home in Perth with family and friends, and then I would move across to start the New Year in a new city. It was to have been the holiday or the long service that I'd never had. I wanted to pack up my house at my own pace, because I knew the process was going to be an emotional thing. It was my first home, I had bought it with my ex-husband. There was a lot of years to pack up in there and a lot of cleaning up to do.

However, about two-and-a-half, maybe three weeks after I finished up at WA Netball, I received a phone call from John. He went over it all with me again about how he ended up in hospital in Brisbane, had the surgery, then checked out within 24 hours, watched the cricket and flew home. But I knew all of that.

What my fiancé had neglected to tell me in those chats was that when he got back to Sydney he had gone to a specialist and had some more tests. By the time he phoned me, John knew the results of those tests, but for a few days he didn't tell me what those results were.

When I think back over this time, I sometimes I get so mad at him, because I wanted to be there for him. But at other, calmer times I think, If I was in that position, I would probably want my own space as well, just to come to grips with my situation and to figure out how the hell I was going to approach it.

John sat on the news of his testicular cancer. He didn't even confide in his family, his Mum or his Dad, and he is so close to them. But I'm not going to get too mad about that; it was his call. And we were certainly there for him when he finally did tell us.

I can't even contemplate how John felt.

When he finally told me, over the phone, a few days after that strange call when he retold the story of his surgery in Brisbane, I couldn't say a thing.

I did hear what he said. The word. Cancer. I heard it, I think I comprehended it.

But I didn't know what to say. I fumbled for the right words, and then fell back on my beliefs. I'm such a firm believer in attitude, which is one of the reasons John and I are together. Humour and attitude. My response, what I know best in stressful situations, was to quickly go into 'coach' mode. After that long pause, I said to John, 'We will be okay. We'll . . . we'll do this . . . we'll beat it. You just got to remember now, more than ever, that you have to draw on your attitude.'

When I think of this phone conversation now, I get a quiver in my throat and a tear in my eye. John quietly replied, 'Yeah, we will.' But he was angry, he was hurt, he was upset, all with good reason – not at me, at fate, at life. And, he was scared – really, really, really scared.

John had been dealing with it in his own way for a few days, but he'd had some time to get his head around it. For me at that moment, Perth might have been in another universe, so far was it from Sydney. I felt so far away and was so alone. And still I didn't know quite what to say.

'I'll give you some time,' John said tearfully, 'and I'll call you back.'

'I don't know what to say,' I admitted in a whispered voice. 'Just give me a minute.' So we ended the conversation. Our second chat, soon after, was little different.

I wasn't crying, I was just very numb. If you're the coach, to really help your charges you need to give them something constructive – options, strategies, tactics.

I opened up one of my favourite books, *You Can Heal Your Life* by Louise Hay. Cancer; Hay's message was that it was related to things being squashed in your inner being, to lots of pent-up negativity and anger and resentment. Turn that around and you can beat it. I'm sure that explanation wouldn't fly in the face of traditional medicine, but I do believe that people's minds and attitudes can overcome so many things.

As I read that book again, I thought that Hay's words were written especially for John. He has had to go through so much, had such an emotional rollercoaster of a life. You couldn't blame him for having angry feelings and negative feelings locked up inside.

I went straight to my office desk and made up a 'flyer' for us. I put at the very top, in large bold letters, 'Present Perfect'. I was telling myself, 'At this moment we are okay. Instead of expending our energy on "could haves", "should haves" and "might bes", let's stay focused on where we are right now and be truly grateful for that. Then we will live the next moment and the next one and the next one. God willing, there will be many more moments.'

On that flyer I wrote down the definition of 'present perfect' and then I wrote a couple of strategies, exactly as a coach would. And remember, you don't enter into a game of elite sport unless you intend to win.

When I'd finished that flyer, I phoned and said, 'John, this is what I've done; this is a sheet I've put together and this is what's on the sheet. What do you reckon?'

He just went, 'Yeah, yeah.'

I remember tears, I remember crying. John was focused on his thoughts, his emotions. I remember him saying, 'I don't want to die.' He said, 'I don't want my life with you, my intended life with you, not to happen. I want to get married. I want children. I want to live my life. Why me?'

I imagine that John was no different to anybody else in responding to his cancer. From the moment you learn you have cancer, it's a journey. You go numb, then you get hurt and upset and then you get angry. After anger, you have a choice. You can either let what's going on take you over, do nothing about it and fall in a hole, or you can summon up whatever it is you need to deal with it, confront the disease, play the game and do all you can to beat it.

Where was I at this stage? I wasn't angry, I was still in that coach mode. I was upset that he was crying. But in my head was the undying belief that if we were going to beat this, that our mental state was going to be the key to our success.

During that conversation, I said, 'I'm on a plane now, the first plane I can get on I'll be there.' John said, 'No, that's not what I want, what I need is I need some time. I need to get my head around this, I need to figure out what I need to do.'

After a pause, I said, 'I probably need the same . . .

'Remember,' I continued, alluding to the fact that he'd kept the cancer secret for a few days, 'you've had a head start on me.'

After Trish, I told Mum and Dad. My Dad, champion bloke that he is, has always taught me to see the funny side of absolutely everything in life. 'Without that funny side of life, mate,' he'd sometimes say, 'life can be shit.' Crass maybe, but 100 per cent right. You need to see the funny side of absolutely everything.

When I told my Old Man about my testicular cancer, he was clearly a little bit shocked to start with. Then he quietly said, 'Johnno, I can't believe it.'

'*You* can't believe it!' I replied, 'How do you think I feel?'

'I'm totally stunned,' Dad said. 'First of all, it was your legs – boom! They're gone. Now it's your nuts – boom! They're gone. I'll come over next week and all you'll be is a head.'

Thanks, Dad.

I laughed and I cried, but more than that, his comment put a smile on my face. I think from that moment on we were *all* ready to face the weeks ahead together.

When I told my Mum about the cancer, you could have knocked her over with a feather. Here we'd been, fighting and fighting and fighting for the entire 30 years of my life to get me integrated into 'normal' society, and all of a sudden that 'normal' life might be taken away from me in such a brutal way. For a short while, Mum was something of a mess, but typical of her, she dealt with it quietly in her own way and then rebounded to give me all the support I needed.

My treatment got into full swing. More importantly, my mind started working again. My attitude now was to take each day as it comes. They've just given me two years left to live, but I could get hit by a truck tomorrow. Trish underlined this when she told me that the present was perfect. Keep it that way. Present perfect. Day by day.

Trish and I began working on a plan – not a plan to beat the cancer but a life plan. We settled on how our time would be best spent in the future and what was important to us. We decided to get rid of *all* the shit in our lives. Looking back on this, it's funny the way we waited until a potential tragedy hit us before doing that. Why the delay? Well, once we started, we did a thorough job. If we didn't need it, we got rid of it. And life suddenly got so much easier.

I set out to do everything possible to beat the disease, but I never looked beyond stumps on the day I was in. I read up on cancer and surfed the web, cramming for knowledge. I became a junkie for cancer information, looking at everything. An aunt had been diagnosed with leukaemia quite a number of years earlier but is now in remission, so I rang her and asked for some advice.

She said, 'Look, just do what the doctors say, but don't stop living.' And I didn't.

For a while the medicos stuck with their 'You've got two years' line. At one appointment I said to the doc, 'I was a miracle when I was born, and miracles last forever. You know, I was supposed to die the day I was born. I've outlived everyone's expectations – my Mum and Dad's, the doctors, sometimes my own. I'm going to outlive yours.'

Trish van Leeuwen: When you're down you can stay down or you can get up. Not long after John broke the news to me that he'd been told he only had a maximum of two years to live, I revisited that piece of paper, that flyer I'd created that was headed 'Present Perfect'.

To me it was clear. 'I can think about how he won't be here in two years or I can think about the fact that right now he is and we are okay.' So I chose that option, 'Present Perfect'. John, thinking independently, had come to the same conclusion. We made a deal. We'll live this moment, then the next one and the next one and the next one, and we'll string as many of those moments together as possible. And we'll make each one of those moments the best we can.

For John there were lots of tests, specialists and doctors. Every day, every half-day, we had new information, the next piece of the puzzle. A couple of days into the process we were told that the cancer had spread. We weren't just facing the removal of his second testicle; it was in all those other organs. I remember my heart sinking to my big toe. I didn't want to hear that.

It was my turn to be scared. Up until then I hadn't given death a thought, and that's the truth. I hadn't thought of quitting. I hadn't thought of a negative result, because I was in my coach mode. You don't take the field to lose the game. You take it to win. If you're on the field and you think you're going to lose, for God's sake you shouldn't be on the field in the first place.

Finally, once I got myself back together, I thought, Oh well, the rules of the game have just changed. What strategy now? While the game might be tough, we're still going to play like we're going to win.

During this anguish, I rang my father and said, 'John's been diagnosed with cancer.' Dad had been with me through the bust-up of my first marriage, an emotional experience over the previous two years. I could hear in his voice grave concern for John and concern, too, for me, as if he was wondering, 'How do I take the hurt away from my little girl?'

I remember ringing Dad back soon after that first call, to explain how the cancer had spread. My Dad, always the realist, said flatly, 'You know that's not good, don't you?'

'I know. You don't have to be telling me that,' I said.

'This is going to be a tough one, Trishy,' he continued. 'We're here for you. Just be real about it. While I know you're going to be positive, you've also got to know that things might not work out.'

Straight after that conversation was the first time I thought through the consequences of John not making it. He will always be part of my life whether he is here or not, but . . .

And then it came to me, very quickly and strongly, that the reason John and I are together is because neither of us knows how to stay down.

Never did the doctors suggest that there was a chance I might live longer than those 24 months. Not a ten per cent chance, five per cent, one per cent. They must have thought that – the medical world is full of people surviving way longer than they're supposed to – but they never told me. Bloody realists!

But today, as I write these words, I've finished the treatment, everything's going all right. I was officially put in remission in May 2000, which is great news for me. Of course, you're not properly in remission until you've lasted for some years. Still, a sense of peacefulness has come over my soul. With my form of testicular cancer, if they catch it and can treat it, then it's beatable. And I beat it.

I think I was helped by the fact that my pain threshold is so big that I could withstand the worst moments, physical and emotional, of my treatment, and keep coming back for more. Cancer was another challenge in my life – maybe the toughest, maybe not, it was up there – but it was never a hurdle that looked too big or too intimidating. No hurdle is, I know that.

The phone call I made to my parents, to let them know I was in remission, was very, very sweet, let me tell you. 'See, I told you,' Mum said. When I'd told Trish, she did cartwheels across the lounge room, while I just sat there watching her with a very warm glow inside me. 'What's the matter with you? Aren't you happy?' she asked.

'Trish,' I replied, 'I've just been on one of the most emotional rollercoasters of my life. I'm dancing on the inside, but on the outside I'm just soaking it all in.'

Trish van Leeuwen: John came through the door after a visit to the doctor, and he had a look on his face that scared me. He knows something, I thought, but I'm not sure this is what I want to hear.

John seemed really numb. He said, 'I've got some news.' My heart is in my throat at this stage. I love that saying that is attributed to Mother Teresa, 'God never gives you more than you can handle.' I just wish He didn't trust me so much, I thought. What is He going to dish up now? Then John said quietly, without expression, 'I'm in remission.'

I remember looking at him and saying, *'What!'*

He repeated the verdict, 'I'm in remission; it's stopped.'

I couldn't believe my ears. I was thinking, You are kidding! Because, while I was playing this game not to lose, there was always that possibility that we might not win.

There were a few minutes of silence and disbelief and finally I started jumping around and shouting, *'Fantastic! That is terrific!'* I was so happy and so excited. It was a combination of total disbelief and euphoria and – and *Yahoo!* 'We've slogged our guts out for this game and we've won!'

But there was John, just sitting on the couch with no expression on his face. No smile, no nothing! After I had jumped around the house and screamed and yelled and yahooed, I stopped and looked at him and said, 'What's going on?' This would have been the most diabolical joke in history. John said softly, 'Sorry, I'm just coming to grips with it.' He was like that athlete sitting on the sideline after winning a game, really happy inside, but totally and utterly exhausted to the point of being numb because they had given their *all* to win the game. My fiancé was really spent. He had given his all to get that result.

We went into Parramatta that night to a cheap little restaurant and spent 40 bucks on food and alcohol. I'd say three-quarters of that bill was alcohol. He downed a couple of Southern Comforts and I downed a couple of brandies, over a pizza or something, I forget what. We clinked glasses and had our own little celebration dinner. And then we came home, to sleep out of sheer exhaustion.

I wouldn't wish cancer on anybody, and I don't wish tragedy on anybody, but having said this, I wish everybody went through something like we did because what it does is provide the catalyst for a major cleansing. By that I mean you just peel away and remove all the garbage and clutter in your life.

Suddenly, when someone is going to take life away from you, things and people who are important stand out and the rest means nothing.

I'll never forget walking out of the doctor's surgery after being told I was in remission. I just wanted to burst with excitement. The sense of relief at that time was colossal. And the feeling of triumph that I'd beaten it, that I was capable of conquering such a monster. I can take care of myself, no matter what they throw at me. When I closed that doctor's door behind me, I had a huge smile on my face. The receptionist looked over at me; she had been there when I was first told I had cancer and had stormed so angrily out of that same sterile room. Now, she just smiled back and said simply, 'That's better.'

It sure was.

From Heaven to Hell and Back

I RECKON THERE ARE five reasons why Trish married me. No. 5: Trish gets most of the bed. No. 4: Trish gets almost all the hanging space in the wardrobe. No. 3: Trish can't get tinea. No. 2: What's a woman's favourite hobby? Easy, it's shopping. And where do you park when you take a disabled person shopping? And No. 1? From what I understand, every young lady wants a man who can stand up and his willy drags on the ground.

We had our moments in the two years between when we got engaged and when Trish came over to live with me in Sydney, and I'm not talking about the awful times during my cancer battle. Gee, it was tough, just the fact that she was living so far away. Telstra loved us.

Trish van Leeuwen: The night of the day we learnt John was in remission was the time we set a wedding date. I would have married John anyway, whether he was in remission or not, but we had made the choice to fight one battle at a time. We kept it very small – 35 people on a boat on Sydney Harbour – our bridal party, our immediate families and half a dozen close friends each. This meant, of course, that many special friends weren't on board, but they are all still special, and I hope they understood.

Just to confirm that we hadn't lost our sense of humour, as people were boarding the boat, we played the theme to *The Love Boat*. For when we left the wharf, we'd contemplated playing the theme from *Titanic*, but settled instead for the theme to *Gilligan's Island*!

The day we got married – words can't explain my emotions. I wasn't feeling able-bodied on my wedding day. I wasn't feeling disabled either. I was just feeling like John Coutis. All the goals I've ever set for myself – to never take second best, to live life, to be me – were embodied in this day; I could see how far I'd come. I thought back to when I'd just assumed that I would be living my adult life by myself. Now I was breaking *all* the rules. How my life had changed. I wanted to pinch myself, 'Wake up'. It was more than a dream come true.

When I clambered onto the boat, the first thing I did was go straight up to the wedding cake, which was sitting there proudly for all to see. There was no doll pushed into the cake. It was a real groom doll that Trish had had specially made – without legs, the way she sees me. For some people, that might not have meant much. To me, it was incredibly special.

Steve Waugh: I was honoured to be asked to be Johnno's best man. I was pleased that he picked me and I was really happy for him on the day. He's said to me a few times that he didn't think he'd ever be lucky enough to find his perfect woman, but he's certainly done that. They're a very good match. For him, it's a dream come true. I remember him one day, talking about the old Moving Pictures song, 'What About Me?' He used to think it was about him, that no one took any notice of him. Now he's certainly had his day. He thought getting married was the greatest thing of all time. It really was special for him and his family. Life's turned out great for him.

This, I thought, is where I want to be. To have Trish there, right by my side, was perfect. To have Mum and Dad there, that was a magic moment for me because they could never have thought that all their efforts would come to this, that I'd get married. They always believed that I'd be living with them for the rest of my life. My younger brother and sister were there, too; it was great for them and a proud moment for them, too. Unfortunately Adam couldn't get over from WA, which was a shame, but he sent his very best wishes.

It was in so many ways such a family occasion. Not only did I go through shit during my early years, so did they, on my behalf. They always stood by me. I was so honoured that my closest friends could be there. I would have loved to have had hundreds more on that boat, but we didn't want to do it like that. We did it our way, a simple way.

Like I said, it was perfect.

The only downer on my wonderful wedding day was that I was feeling a bit crook during it. The earliest I can remember being off-colour was after I sneezed in the week leading up to the big day – I thought I'd hurt the muscles in my back. I didn't worry about it at first, but it kept nagging at me, to the point that I told Stephen and my groomsman, Paul Dyett, before the buck's night. When Stephen asked me what I wanted to do, I said emphatically that there was no way I was postponing the wedding. 'If I'd spent my life putting off things,' I told him, 'I'd never have got anything done. I'll just put up with the pain.'

Then on the Friday night, during the buck's night, I had a coughing fit and did my back completely. It was really sore. But she'll be right; I took a couple of Panadols and tried not to worry about it.

I managed to get a really good night's rest but woke up still in some pain. Throughout the day I didn't want people to see the anguish on my face, but you can tell from the wedding photos that I'm sore, especially those happy snaps when I'm sitting on the back of the bar. For the rest of the time, I tried to keep myself suspended, with my butt off the ground and my back straight. Otherwise it was just too painful. But I was okay. I ran on the adrenalin of the day, on my great feelings of pride and joy. The drinks didn't hurt either.

I wasn't thinking 'cancer', that it had come back. I knew what the cancer felt like and this was totally different. I was thinking that it was a nerve or muscle thing. All was okay until after the guests left and I was able to relax. Then the adrenalin left me and my body went bang! I fell asleep, exhausted by it all, and when I woke the next morning I knew that I was in trouble. I couldn't move properly.

I lasted through the rels coming over to our house for the present opening, even made it to stumps that night, but as I got into bed with my bride I remarked to her, 'Darl, my back is a bit bloody sore.'

Trish knew me well enough to know that if I said something was sore then it *was* sore. 'Do you want me to take you to a hospital?' she asked.

'No, no,' I replied, 'I'll be okay.'

But at two o'clock I woke up in sheer agony. I gave Trish a nudge (actually, it was a bit more than a nudge) and said, 'You've got to take me to the hospital *now*.'

Trish quickly put a bag together, while I somehow got myself off the bed, outside and into the car. That wasn't easy. I wasn't going back to where I'd been so poorly treated with the misdiagnosed urinary tract infection, instead I insisted Trish take me to a private hospital where I knew I would get looked after. The doc there admitted, 'Look, we don't really know what to do but we'll give you a good dose of painkillers, get you to sleep and see what happens.'

The next day I was treated by Dr Stephen Parsons, a GP who specialises in sleep apnoea and one of the best doctors I've ever met in my life. By the time he saw me my back was so tender that I couldn't handle the slightest touch on it. I couldn't even handle water running down it. It's what they call 'hypersensitive'. I call it 'hell'.

Dr Parsons was up front with me. 'John,' he said slowly, 'we don't know what's the matter with you.' The simplest tasks were taking an eternity. I had no idea how long I was going to be in there. A shower involved two hours of hell, to get out of the bed, walk 10 metres, get into the shower, out of the shower, back 10 metres, back into bed. And I wasn't on my own during those two hours, I had three people assisting me. I had no independence. I was just like a baby – going to the toilet was impossible without someone to help me get on and off.

The indignity of it all.

And no one knew what was wrong. Just two days after the best time of my life, I felt as if I'd lost everything.

'If there's anything more that I've got to get through this year,' I cried to Trish one night, 'I'll be a mental case.'

I reckon I've had my fair share of pain and setbacks and hardship over 31 years. I'd had enough – for the first time in my life, that's what I was thinking. I want to go and spend some time with my wife. I've just got married, I shouldn't be in hospital, I should be off partying. If this was the Big Fella upstairs testing me again, this time He'd gone a bit too far.

The doctors were speculating that the problem was nerve-related. They instigated so many tests, stuck needles in here and here and here, took so much blood Dracula would have been proud of me, filled me up with pills, hooked me up with drips and wires, put heat pads on my back, stuck some vibrating machine on me. That machine! They put it on me one day while Mum was visiting, and while the nurse was elsewhere, Mum – who is, of course, a nurse – decided it wasn't going hard enough. She hit the volume switch and – *Mum!* – my eyes were popping out of my head. And still no one knew what was wrong with me.

Originally I was in a ward with around six or seven other patients, but when it became apparent that I was going to be there for a while, they gave me a room of my own. I really appreciated this move, but it meant that there were times when I had no company, that I could lie there on my own, every movement painful, with nothing to do but contemplate a future like this.

I had rearranged my room to the way that I wanted it, with my bed next to the window. Outside it was a beautiful day. I mean, every day is beautiful but this was one of Mother Nature's special ones. Cars buzzed up and down the road, people walked along the streets, some late, some strolling. From what I could see, none of these people, drivers or pedestrians, had a problem or a care in the world. And here was I, two storeys above them, thinking to myself, I can't handle this any more, I've had enough. I was ready to throw the white towel in. 'This isn't what my life is about,' I told myself. 'This is not what my life is meant to be.' No one could tell me what was the matter with me. I couldn't even get out of bed.

'If I'm in a bed for the rest of my life,' I sobbed to myself late one night, 'I'll kill myself.'

This thought went against everything I had ever believed and taught and preached. I knew that. But if I was going to be stuck in a bloody bed, that wouldn't be a good life for Trish. That's not why we got married.

I was deeply depressed because I did not know what was wrong. I hated it when Trish came to see me in the state I was in; I hated it when the nurses came into the room to take care of me, to wash me, to feed me.

I would have been hell to visit, but my good friends stuck by me. Then Alan Jones, God bless him, organised for a specialist from Brisbane to fly down and check me out, after someone phoned Alan to tell him that I was struggling. That specialist, Professor Dan, asked for some more X-rays, to add to the ever-expanding book of J. Coutis X-rays the hospital was compiling.

Even before he came to see me, Professor Dan had gone to radiology to have a look at the scans and X-rays that had already been taken. To capture the scene, you need to know that Professor Dan looks a lot like the famous Professor Julius Sumner Miller, with mannerisms to match.

Here he is, staring at these X-rays stuck up on the screen, nose up close to the light. He can't work it out. He's sticking different slides up here and there, looking at different angles. I've seen those X-rays – they make my body look like a leg of lamb from a butcher's shop. 'What the hell is this?' he asked as he turned to the doctors standing behind him. And this, in a nutshell, was the problem. No one had seen a body like mine, with the spine at an ugly angle and only going about half as far down my back as it was supposed to. My rib cage is incomplete. Because there is no backbone in the lower part of my back, the nerves and the lower part of my spinal cord are all over the place. If you cut me right through the guts from front to back or side to side you'd never hit any bone. All the vital organs work, but they're not all where they should be. My body has got me this far, and I'm hoping and wishing it'll get me a lot further, but in this radiology room Professor Dan asked again, 'What is this?'

Finally he came up to see me, took one look, clicked his fingers as any good professor should, and smiled at me and said, 'I wish they'd told me earlier. I'll be back in a minute.' In a very short time he was able to work out what hours and hours of meetings involving any number of eminent specialists couldn't. But please don't think I'm dirty on those specialists – they treated me magnificently. It was just that they'd never seen a body like mine. Professor Dan might have been the only doctor in the whole wide world who could have made this particular 'two plus two' add up to four.

I had been in hospital for two-and-a-half weeks before Professor Dan came and worked out what was needed. It *was* a nerve problem. His game plan was to inject some painkilling alcohol into my back to try to locate the nerves, then determine which of them were damaged, and then work out how awful that damage might be. The process was going to be a slow one, basically nerve by nerve, down the back until he hit the one or ones that were causing my extreme pain. If the painkiller hit a nerve that wasn't damaged, then it would make no difference to my discomfort.

So encouraging and confident was the professor that the further we got into the process, even though this involved more and more injections, the better, in my mind, I felt. Finally, boom, he struck gold, found the damaged nerve and, just like that, the pain was gone.

Seriously, I leapt out of bed. Before that I hadn't been able to get out of bed for two-and-a-half weeks. Now I ran up and down the hallway, knocking into walls and slurring my yahoos as I did so because I was full of dope.

This was the first part of the process. Having isolated the nerve that was causing me all this grief, they continued for about a fortnight to inject painkillers into it. And then, as a much more long-term solution, and having worked out there would be no nasty side effects, they deadened the nerve.

Steve Waugh: The problem was that all the doctors had never seen a body like his. That was the hardest thing for John. Even when he was being diagnosed he was learning stuff about his own body that he'd never been told before. Early days, I rang

John a couple of times a day to see how he was going. I felt for the first time ever that he was down and negative about things. Understandably so, as he'd just had the best day of his life and now he couldn't move, couldn't even go to the toilet, he was in absolute agony. But a lot of his friends rallied behind him, and gradually you could see him pick up his spirits.

From the moment I knew that someone might be able to fix me, my depression left me. There was a way out. There always is, I should have remembered that. My recovery became a challenge for me and, as I've said many, many times, all challenges are positive. Unfortunately, though, my heartache wasn't over yet.

On the Friday after the operation that deadened that bloody nerve, my Dad called me. 'John, I know you're crook in hospital,' he said, 'but I need to tell you that Mum has had a heart attack.'

Straightaway I burst into tears. I'd been told I needed to stay in the hospital for at least the entire weekend but I couldn't pack my bag quickly enough. There was no way I was going to be able to get up to where my parents live, about five or six hours drive north of Sydney, to see her, but there was no way in the world I was staying in hospital either.

Bags packed, I rang Trish and said, 'You've got to come and get me. Mum's had a heart attack.' Trish was immediately on her way.

The doctors said, 'No, no, no, you can't go.'

'I'm sorry, I've got to go.' I was defiant.

'Okay then,' they responded. 'But please, stay at home. Don't go anywhere. You need to rest.' They further underlined that point to Trish when she arrived to collect me.

I was getting too many reminders that life is too short. I wanted to get home and get on with mine. They wanted me to stay in hospital so that the nurses could take care of me, but I didn't go home for Trish to take care of me, I went home to get back to my life. Mum's just had a heart attack; I'm waiting to hear from Dad; they've taken her to the hospital; I've rung the hospital, 'I'm sorry Mr Coutis, we don't have any information at this stage.'

It was a terrifying period in my life. To think that my Mum could be gone – I started crying, I was a wreck again. This wasn't someone from down the street, a name in the paper; this was my Mum, my guardian angel, who'd looked after me for 31 years. I needed her to be there for a lot longer.

At the hospital Mum had been admitted to, they did all the tests through the Saturday, and on the Sunday Dad rang me to say that they'd got the results back and it was angina. Thank God for that. It was still a bad thing but it wasn't a heart attack. The peacefulness that came over my soul at that moment was immense.

Mum's road to recovery started that day, and so did mine. There were still some hiccups with my physical state, but gradually, ever gradually, I worked my way back to good health. Now, as I write this, I'm as fit as the proverbial fiddle, and Mum is, too. But I must say this – although all the doctors, nurses and staff were wonderful to me, if I had my way, I'd never go to another bloody hospital again.

A World of Legs

DURING 2000, ONE OF the places I was invited to speak was at a conference in country Victoria. In the audience were 450 cattlemen from around Australia, plus international guests who included, I soon found out, some good Irish folk.

As is my custom after any of my presentations, when I finished I asked for questions and comments from the floor. Immediately, one fellow jumped to his feet.

'Mr Coutis,' he began in a thick Irish brogue, 'me name is Michael Magan. I'd just like t'say that, after t'night, I'll be able to ring m'son this even'n and tell 'im I've met me first true real giant this day.'

Afterwards Mike sought me out and we had a long chat. He spoke about getting me to Ireland, to speak to audiences over there. 'Organise that,' I told him, 'and Trish and I'll be on the plane.'

Sure enough, a few months later Mike was on the phone to tell us that the chance to speak in Ireland had materialised. But there was, sadly, an awful twist. Mike's son had been diagnosed with a brain tumour, and Mike was now totally committed to raising money for cancer research. The speaking program he had arranged had me on the bill for a major fundraiser he was organising in Dublin. As well, there would be opportunities to speak to school children. Would we come? Of course we would. First to Ireland then on to London for a few days holiday.

I had been overseas a few times, but never had I been as excited as this. Previously I had spoken on stages in Mauritius, Singapore and Kuala Lumpur. In Kuala Lumpur I found myself up on-stage in a football stadium in front of more than 30,000 people. Mauritius had been an eye-opener. We stayed at a glamorous six-star resort, as luxurious as anything I've encountered, but we also ventured to a market where the locals' reaction to me was so aggressive and ill-tempered that I honestly feared for my life. It was as if I was some sort of evil demon that had to be cast away; I'll never forget the look of hatred in their eyes as they tried to corner me. My understanding is that disabled people are seen as grotesque and are thus kept out of view over there; when I appeared in that market it rattled them, and they reacted the way they did. They were hopelessly ill-informed about people with disabilities, so perhaps I should forgive them – but, geez, the look in their eyes.

England in December 2000, being the sophisticated place it was, would not be like that Mauritius market. We checked into our hotel, which was located in a quiet cul-de-sac just 150 metres away from the front doors of one of London's finest shopping venues. Once we'd had a bit of a wash and a lie down, Trish and I grinned at each other and said 'Okay, let's go shopping!'

On the stroll down to this store, I was in such high spirits I couldn't help but share my good fortune with passers-by. 'G'day, how are ya?' I laughed in the thickest North Richmond accent I could muster. 'What a beautiful day.' Some chuckled; most just ignored me; a couple pulled their scarves and beanies over their faces. I loved it.

And then, there it was. Shopping heaven. Because I'd put my skateboard into top gear, when I got to the impressive store entrance I had to wait for Trish and one of our friends, Nick, to catch up. Finally they arrived and in we went.

'I'm sorry, ma'am,' the security man on the door said as we walked in, 'he can't come in on that.'

Pardon? Are you talking to me?

No, he wasn't. He was talking *about* me. He was talk-ing to Trish.

'I'm sorry, he can't come in on that board.'

'If you've got a problem with me,' I roared, 'then talk to me!'

'You'll have to hold it there, sir,' he looked down at me. 'You can't come in here.'

And then he looked up at Trish and said again, 'He can't come in here.'

He was a tall fellow, youthful and wiry, a younger version of Basil Fawlty. And very sure of himself. I couldn't cope with the fact that he wouldn't talk to me, as if I was some sort of pet and he was better off talking to the owner. This was not what I had imagined England to be.

'Mate, if you've got a problem with me,' I repeated angrily, 'you talk to me. I've taken this skateboard with me everywhere. It's my legs. Are you telling me I can't come in here?'

'I'm sorry, sir, you can't come in here,' he said again smugly. 'The store policy is that you need to be in a wheelchair.'

At this point we were joined by a second security guard, who confirmed that it was indeed store policy for me to be in a wheelchair. At least this bloke looked at me as he spoke, but he did so from his full height, the distance from his nose to mine making me feel that he was talking down to me in more ways than one.

'Why don't we just find you a wheelchair?'

If my wife hadn't been with me at this moment, I would have done one of two things. I would have either told them what to do with their wheelchair and walked out, or I would have thrown my skateboard right through their grand bloody entrance. I was so angry. Instead I stood and argued my case, as people stopped in the entrance and the street outside to see what was going on. And then the phone behind the security man's desk rang.

'Hello . . . Ah, yes, sir . . . No sir . . . Yes, certainly, sir. Ah, sir, ma'am, sir. Please go in.'

I can only assume that someone very senior had been watching what was going on via the security cameras and realised that what was happening was not doing any good for the store's image. So in we proudly went, saying nothing to these security boofheads when there was so much I wanted to shout. The store was very overrated, though maybe we weren't in the mood to be impressed. And throughout I watched the security cameras as they followed my every move. Or so it seemed.

In its own way, this experience was just as distressing as my time in that Mauritius market. In fact, because I had expected so much more from the Poms, it was in many ways worse.

This was a low point in our trip, but otherwise we had a fantastic time. Absolutely nothing else went even remotely wrong. Mike's fundraising night in Dublin was a phenomenal success. This one man with his dreams and goals raised over £170,000. In one night! And there are many more fundraisers to come. Mike is doing a remarkable job, let me tell you.

The audience that evening included a wide variety of people from the local community. It was a mainly adult audience, and when I went out on-stage it took me a little while to get going. I was an unknown quantity, and I don't think they knew how to react to me. I cracked a couple of jokes that would have won a laugh back home, but here there was nothing. Once I broke the ice, though, we were away. I learnt a lot that night about talking to a foreign audience, and hopefully the people in the audience learnt a little as well.

I also spoke at a few schools in Longford, which is about two hours drive south-west of Dublin. This is where Mike's family live. We spoke at both his daughter's school and his son's high school. These visits went really, really well, to the point that I was mobbed when I finished. I had never evoked that kind of response before in my life. I felt like one of the Backstreet Boys, especially at Mike's daughter's school, where there were, fair dinkum, something like 600 girls aged about 14 to 17 who rushed the stage to get an autograph.

I didn't expect such a reception, but I did enjoy it. Sure it was good for the ego, but more importantly it meant I'd made an impact. The students at the boys school weren't quite so excited, but very enthusiastic all the same.

Earlier in the trip, as a promotion for the Dublin fundraiser, I did an interview on one of Ireland's leading radio stations. The next day, when I strolled down the street, I was stopped time and again for an autograph or a photo. This told me two things – that my message could have an impact anywhere and that, like Australians, the Irish are willing to accept people with disabilities and recognise that the disabled want to live 'normal' lives and are perfectly capable of doing so.

In all, we spent eight days in Ireland. There were many

times, both in Ireland and before that in London, when I was thinking, This is a long, long way from North Richmond.

Another time I had that same thought was during one of my visits to Perth to see Trish in the days when she was still living there. I was driving, maybe a touch too fast, down the Kwinana Freeway. It was pouring with rain and then I was pulled over by the police. Because of the weather, I wasn't going to get out of the car, so I watched in my rear-vision mirror as a young constable stepped out into the storm, put his hat on and ran towards me. You could tell by his body language that he was none too thrilled about having to be out in the rain. He looked like he was thinking, Write the ticket and get outta here. As he tapped on my window he was already opening his pad, ready to write the details he needed. I wound down the window. 'Sir,' he said before looking up, 'you were speeding.'

Then he looked into the car. His speech stopped mid-sentence, and he was left, mouth open, stumbling to come out with anything. Finally he mumbled, 'Please don't do that again,' and with that he turned, ticket unwritten, and ran back out of the rain.

I watched the constable get in his car and his partner clearly ask, 'What happened?' Instead of answering, however, my 'interrogator' slumped over the steering wheel, shaking his head.

I guess I wasn't the criminal he'd been expecting.

Tom O'Toole: I remember once we went into this restaurant, John and I, and he was so loud. I thought enough people were looking at us anyway. I said, 'John, why you gotta be so loud?' He said, 'Tom, when I'm this bloody little, I gotta make a noise or I'll never get served.'

The way police officers and everyone else sees me has changed from how it used to be – though try explaining that to that security guard in London! When I was growing up, many Australians assumed that because I had such a major physical disability, I was severely mentally disabled as well. I would have people approaching me and shouting, or talking to me as if I was a one year old about to utter my first fair-dinkum word. Or they'd speak slowly, very slowly. At other times, I'd get people coming up to me as if I was someone's pet. They'd pat me on the head and call me 'Little Fella'. Nine times out of ten, I'd play the dill. I'd sit there and look at these misguided people, as if I was trying to understand them but couldn't quite make anything of it, until one of my mates would come up and say g'day to me and I'd start up a normal conversation. The people who'd been talking very slowly would slink away as quick as they could.

I know that acting as if I *was* mentally retarded was a very juvenile thing to do. One day, my grandmother caught me doing this and gave me a good hiding. But, geez, it used to piss me off, the way they'd go on. Today these people are harder to find, but it still happens.

Steve Waugh: John has taught me plenty of things. Patience is one thing; not to take yourself too seriously is another. I've learnt this from the way he takes on the chin comments from others that were supposed to have been made out of earshot. That's just a part of his life, as it is for me in a different sort of way, and I admire the manner in which he just gets on with living and doesn't worry about what people say or what they think. I also admire the way he gives everything and everyone a go.

The change in facilities for disabled people has been significant. Back in the 1970s, there were next to no facilities for us. As I've said, before I could start at my first 'able-bodied' school, Dad had to build some ramps and make a few minor adjustments to the toilets. It's funny when you think that there was absolutely no wheelchair access to so many areas; this meant that there was no pram access either, so it wasn't just discrimination against the disabled. Nowadays, of course, there are ramps on nearly every corner, so it's not only this baby who can get around so much better. It's still bloody hard, though, to use an ATM machine, and it's tricky to park your wheelchair at a table in a fast-food restaurant if the chairs around that table are fixed to the floor.

Back in the 'olden' days, the early-to-mid-'80s, when things were tougher for people in wheelchairs, I was lucky because I often didn't need a chair to get around. I had my skateboard. But I'd been in a wheelchair often enough to recognise barriers that the community had unknowingly built that hampered the disabled. And, of course, I have plenty of mates in wheelchairs who are in a lot of trouble if they are confronted by a set of stairs, even a couple of steps or a steep gutter. Because of these barriers, many able-minded people were confined to their homes; what a shame that just a few short years ago society made little effort to get them out into the real world.

In my time, I've watched the relationship between the able-bodied and the not-so-able-bodied in Australia grow, then split a bit, grow some more, split a bit again, then grow some more. The sum of this process has been progress; there's no doubt that we're all on the right track but there is also no doubt that there is still much to be done.

Public transport for disabled people must be improved. And, in my view, industry and government should develop many more opportunities in the workplace for disabled people, and give more disabled people a go in jobs that they've been kept away from in the past. Australia is the fairest country in the world, but we can be even better. We need to learn to give deserving people a pat on the back for having a go. We should also give even more people an opportunity to have a go themselves.

> **Gavin Robertson:** I've heard John say lots of times, 'Get out there and have a go. If you win, you win, if you lose, you lose; if you lose just accept it. Either way, it's good, because otherwise you sit inside on your arse doing nothing.'

One of my greatest hopes is that all people with disabilities will be viewed by Australians simply as human beings, capable of being as honest, loving and hardworking as the able-bodied person standing next to them. We're not looking for charity, and don't want to be seen as a charity. The Paralympics, for example, were seen by many observers as a charity, when it was actually an event for elite sportspeople. Happily, a lot more sports fans were aware of that fact by the time the Paralympics were over. Hopefully, they'll all remember.

I understand there are many types of disabilities and degrees of disability, but we all have hearts in our chests, blood in our veins and a brain in our heads, so why should we automatically be seen as being different? Of course, much of this comes back to how disabled people see themselves. I would love the disabled, no matter what their age or what their disability, to see themselves as capable of getting out there and having a go; as being able to make a difference to their own lives. There's the old saying, 'God helps those who help themselves'; I believe there's a large number of disabled individuals who need to get off their arses, and get out there and help themselves. Give it a go. I'm not saying it's easy, but we've all got dreams. This goes for everyone, but just as much for the disabled. Write those dreams down and turn them into goals. No matter who you are, what you are, where you live, what you do – only you can discover what your body is capable of. Come on, you can do it.

If I can, you can.

I live in a world of legs, high-heeled shoes, sneakers, work boots, footy socks, foot odour, knee braces, jeans, bulging back pockets with enormous wallets in them, short skirts and g-strings, hairy legs, shaved legs and all kinds of legs in between. My world is a world of many different things, but mostly legs. And cats and dogs, getting caught in grass, and drowning in puddles that look little but turn into swimming pools when you walk through them.

I can tell a lot from people's shoes – where they've been, why they've been there, where they're going, how they're going to get there, even their age – all from their footwear. What sort of work they do, what kind of social life they lead. You can't tell from working boots how hard those people work, but the scuff marks on business shoes reveal how much pride people take in themselves, while you can tell from the quality of running shoes (and socks!) just how fair dinkum the athletes are.

My physical make-up means some things are a lot trickier for me than they are for others. Bouncers like throwing me out of nightclubs because they can toss me such a long way. And I don't like Mauritius marketplaces or big dogs either. If they're off their leashes, big dogs might send a little shiver up the spines of adults. They terrify me.

What do I like about my disability? Most of all, I like the fact that I'm now in a position to help the world change so it is better able to cope with disabled people. I like the doors my disability – or more specifically, I guess, my attitude to my disability – have opened for me. I do play on it every now and then. To be honest, when I was younger, I used to play on it all the time, but as you get older you learn what is right and what isn't. Still, I'm the first to acknowledge that I wouldn't have been invited to go on tour with the Australian cricket team if it hadn't been for my disability, I wouldn't get the opportunity to speak at a variety of functions and meet some brilliant people, I wouldn't have met my wife, and so on and so on.

One of the things I worry about the most is that my body will wear out. I'm just hoping that it won't. I would love to be able to confidently look forward to another 30 or 40 years of life; if my body can do that then I will have had a good run. I do need to ensure that my diet stays healthy and that I am careful with what I do and where I go. When I was younger, I just went and did whatever I wanted to without any fear, but if I want to see a few more decades I can't do that any more.

One thing I will never know is what my life would have been like if I had been born with legs that worked properly. I don't want to know; it doesn't interest me at all. Today I have no legs. I am John Coutis.

My situation has taught me that we, as individuals, need to stand up for what we believe in. There are some mongrel people in this world who will always knock you down and treat you badly. I've had to really believe in myself and back myself to get to where I am today. I've had to fight and fight and fight, just to get my message across, that I can be someone despite my disability. I could have taken it easy, I could have sat at home and done nothing, but, with my Mum and Dad's help, I – no, we – chose not to. We chose to take on the world.

> **Liberty Coutis:** First and foremost he has become himself. He's not frightened to do anything.

Because I never stop to feel sorry for myself, I don't have any major emotional or psychological problems. And because I've accepted my situation, I never have to look back; I'm forever looking forwards, which I'm sure is the way to go.

> **Evelyn Coutis:** I like to walk behind him. He goes along on his skateboard, and the crowd parts from him, and I walk along close behind and then they fall in behind us. I find that fascinating how they part, it's almost as if he's God. But the truth is that they'll get run over if they don't get out of the way.

I'd like the world to see John Coutis as a fun-loving, warm, caring larrikin, someone who likes to have a beer with his mates. I'd like the world to see John Coutis as someone who's fair, someone who will try to help people. And if he can't do that himself, he'll go to the trouble of finding somebody who can. I'd like the world to see John Coutis as an Australian, as a human being, as somebody who gets out there and has a go and won't let anything stop him. I'd like the world to see John Coutis as someone who not just makes a difference, but also has an impact on people. I'd like John Coutis to touch hundreds of thousands of people before his life is through. Hopefully, this simple story will change some lives.

On New Year's Eve at the end of 1999, I decided to write down my goals. It's a process I do from time to time. My top goal was straight to the point: 'I will become the greatest disabled speaker of all time within ten years.'

After I wrote that I looked at it but it wasn't right. However, I couldn't work out what was wrong. I put down the paper on which I'd written that goal, walked away and left it for about two hours. When I came back and looked at it, the error hit me right in the face. 'That's not right,' I said out loud, 'I've got to take out one word.'

Disabled.

Now that goal reads, 'I will become the greatest speaker of all time within ten years.'

My Dad often said, 'You know, Johnno, you've got to find something that you love doing and then do it well. Be the best you can be at it and then find a way to get paid for doing it.'

When I look at what I'm doing now, I think, hey, I am following my Dad's doctrine. I absolutely love what I'm doing these days – the public speaking, the interaction with all sorts of people, the feeling I'm making a difference to others. I miss that interaction when I don't do it; I get withdrawal symptoms, like a kid who hasn't had an ice-cream for a while.

I owe plenty of people plenty, but I do what I do for me.

I want those who have helped me, supported me, had confidence in me, to be proud of me. I do what I do to show that disabled people – which, remember, is everybody – can do anything. I do what I do because I love a challenge. I do what I do because I want to be different, I want to be out of the norm. I do what I do because so many people don't get the chance to do what they want to do. In my heart, I believe I have the power to make lives change (including my own), and I want to use that power.

I've always wanted to become a great speaker, not just a good one. I want to be remembered for my message and the way that message can change people's lives. I've been told I have a rare gift and that is to be able to change the attitude of some people in an audience, simply by jumping up on stage and speaking honestly and passionately. Every time I get up on stage, I have a chance to make an impact. And, at the same time, I have the opportunity to enjoy a personally rewarding experience. This is why I want to be an excellent speaker.

People who know me know that I set my goals high. Whether I can reach that goal, only time will tell, but I do know that anything is possible. You watch me. After all, I reckon I'm living proof that, if you so desire, there's no such word as 'can't'. I *am* a little different. I do have a disability, but I won't let that prevent me from doing what I like, when I like, how I like it.

Mine is not a story of an individual leading a 'normal' (whatever that is) existence, but then suffering a huge life-threatening setback before fighting back to normality and beyond. My problems started at birth, when my parents were told I wasn't going to make it. I literally had to fight from the ground up. To get to the point where I could earn a modicum of independence, even look after myself, get myself around, live under my own roof – if I'd stopped there, that would have been an achievement. But I had set my sights beyond that. Today I'm having the time of my life, and also trying to help schoolkids and battlers, even business leaders and sporting icons, by simply telling them my story, and explaining some of the tricks of the living trade that I've learnt along my unique journey.

Down here where I am, you discover and appreciate things that shoot straight by most people striding down the street. You learn about love and gratitude, about pain and suffering, about courage and adversity, about life and death, about what can be done. Which is everything.

The trick is to overcome your disability, whatever it might be, and take on life. 'Can't' shouldn't come into it.